Essentially Thai

Spirit House

Essentially Thai

Spirit House

Helen Brierty and Annette Fear

Photography by Graeme Gillies

NH
NEW HOLLAND

Dedication

This book is dedicated to the hundreds of enthusiastic, committed people who have contributed to the success of Spirit House over the years—chefs, waiters, apprentices, kitchen hands, gardeners, office staff, local farmers, fishermen and suppliers. Plus a sincere thanks to all the restaurant diners and cooking school students who so obviously enjoy their Spirit House experience.

Acknowledgements

Chef Annette Fear's recipes are inspired by dozens of trips to Thailand over a 25-year period which, combined with her skill in designing recipes, result in the taste sensations contained within these pages. All the stories relating to each recipe are from Annette's research and travels.

But Annette rarely travels alone. Accompanying her on many tours are senior chefs from the Spirit House restaurant and her fellow teaching chefs Katrina Ryan and Kelly Lord. Our son Acland Brierty, fluent in the Thai language and like us all in love with Thai cuisine, leads the tours. Add to this Spirit House crew a select group of eight adventurous clients who tag along for the tasting ride of a lifetime through Thai streets, canals, markets and restaurants, and enough raw material is there for our chefs, in both restaurant and cooking school, to create recipes that will delight our diners and students.

A special thanks to Katrina and Kelly who cooked and beautifully presented many of these dishes for the photography sessions. Their knowledge, teaching skills and original recipes, so aptly demonstrated over many years, have undoubtedly contributed to the growth, popularity and reputation of the cooking school.

Over five days of the photo shoot, food stylist Jaime Reyes taught us all the tricks of his trade—now we understand why home cooked recipes sometimes don't look anything like their pictures in the book! Photographer Graeme Gillies was a study in patience and has created finished images guaranteed to make you salivate and go wow!

Respect and admiration for restaurant head chef Ben Bertei and his team of 10 chefs, for the great tastes and flavours they offer daily from their smallest of kitchens, and for floor manager Jess da Costa and her energetic staff who provide such efficient, friendly service to clients but still keep smiling while dodging water dragons and other native 'beasties' underfoot. Eileen Roberts in the office, gardener/handyman Mr Fix-it-later Blake Brierty, school assistant Wayan Griffith radiating her Balinese smile and grace—all so valued and appreciated.

Contents

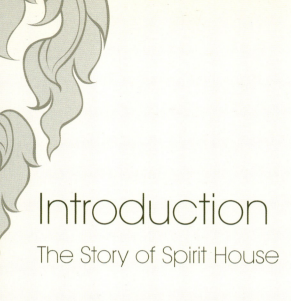

Introduction

The Story of Spirit House

In the early 1980s, my husband Peter and I owned a manufacturing pottery at Montville in Queensland. In response to an increasing demand for large earthen pots, we travelled to Thailand on a research trip and met Suvit Pholvivat, a young Thai student, who became a lifelong family friend.

First and foremost, Suvit was a 'foodie' par excellence! Every business trip to Thailand over the following years was merely an excuse to sip, sup and slurp our way through food markets and explore regional food while drinking countless bottles of Singha beer, as Suvit introduced us to the intricate regional flavours and exotic ingredients of his beloved national cuisine. For our whole family, Thailand became a case of love at first bite.

One memorable trip, driving through a featureless north-east rural area, Suvit turned down a bumpy sidetrack which suddenly opened onto an exquisite Thai restaurant, nestled in rambling tropical gardens overlooking a small lake. The relaxed meal and tranquil restaurant setting stayed permanently impressed on our minds—even though we had long ago vowed we would never open another restaurant.

Fast forward to 1991 when we purchased 2 hectares (5 acres) of flat, bare land at Yandina on Queensland's Sunshine Coast with the dream of replicating that rural Thai dining experience. Everyone questioned the choice of such an isolated rural location, but surrounded by farmers growing ingredients like ginger, galangal, turmeric, green pawpaw (papaya), kaffir limes, lemongrass and chillies, the time and place seemed right to add modern Thai cuisine to the already impressive array of Sunshine Coast dining destinations.

Over the next four years, tropical gardens were designed, ponds excavated, bamboo, palms and understorey planted. As the acreage was transformed, Thai-style buildings, statues and two spirit houses were positioned in the gardens. In October 1995, Spirit House opened its carved red gates.

Word slowly spread about the Asian culinary magic in the kitchen under the creative direction of Annette Fear, our first Head Chef, whose fragrant Thai-inspired food set the standard for the many restaurant chefs who followed her over the years. With the addition of the cooking school in 1998, food tours to Bangkok since 2002, recipe books and food products, Spirit House has gradually evolved into a mecca for lovers of Thai cuisine.

Essentially Thai is the culmination of 15 years working closely with Annette—of shared sweat, tears, highs and lows but above all, much wit, fun and laughter. Our previous books, *Thai Cooking* and *Travels With Thai Food*, demonstrated Annette's gift for creating recipes that demystify classic Thai ingredients and methods while providing home cooks with inspiring dishes. Teaching classes every day gives us a unique insight into how Australian families like to eat and how they want to entertain—fresh, fast and fabulous is our summation! The following recipes certainly deliver on that.

Helen Brierty

Thai Essentials

When the Spirit House restaurant opened in 1995, one of the myriad difficulties we had to overcome to operate a restaurant in a rural area was finding a regular supply of Asian dry goods. The nearest Asian supermarket was 100 kilometres away and the local supermarket's stock of Asian ingredients was limited to a few dusty bottles of soy and oyster sauce.

But how times have changed. Push a trolley through the local supermarket now and whole aisles are devoted to Asian ingredients—Japanese, Korean, Chinese, Thai, Vietnamese, Indonesian and Malaysian cuisines are all represented through a vast array of sauces, pastes, noodles, spices and Asian delicacies in exotically labelled packets, jars and bottles to entice the eye.

With Thai cuisine, there are some basic ingredients which are used in most recipes. Stock up your pantry with the following essentials and you will always have on hand the keys to unlocking the taste of Thai.

Essential Pastes

Pastes are the building blocks of Thai cuisine. They can range from a simple blend of coriander (cilantro) roots and stems, pounded together with garlic, through to complex mixtures of aromatic herbs, vegetables and spices which form the basis of Thai curries.

As your cooking skills increase, you can widen your repertoire of pastes, but the following five cover a multitude of applications and should always be kept on hand. There are many brands to choose from, but avoid curry pastes containing preservatives, which tend to add a bitter flavour. After opening, store tightly sealed jars of paste in the refrigerator. To avoid contaminating the contents, always use a clean spoon when removing paste from the jar. Better still, make your own pastes in double quantities and freeze in ice cube trays so that you always have fresh pastes on hand.

Chilli Paste

Makes 2 cups
Chilli paste is very versatile, and can be used in Tom Yum soups, stir-fries and many salad dressings. Often this paste is called roasted chilli paste or chilli jam. While you can make the paste yourself, the commercial varieties are just as good and will save you time. Look for 'chilli paste with soy bean oil' in your supermarket. This paste keeps indefinitely stored in an airtight container in the refrigerator.

4 cups (1 L/34 fl oz) vegetable oil for deep-frying
2 cups golden shallots, peeled and sliced
1 cup garlic, peeled and sliced
¼ cup dried prawns (shrimp), rinsed and dried on paper towel
½ cup large dried red chillies, de-seeded (pitted) and chopped
½ cup (125g/4 oz) light palm sugar
¼ cup (60ml/2 fl oz) thick tamarind water
¼ cup (60ml/2 fl oz) fish sauce

Heat oil in a wok to moderate. Cook shallots until golden. Remove with a slotted spoon, drain on a paper towel. Cook garlic until golden. Cook prawns for one minute, remove with a slotted spoon, drain on paper towel. Cook red chillies until they darken, it will only take a minute. Blend to a paste in a food processor, using some of the deep-frying oil to facilitate the paste. Transfer the paste to a saucepan and add the remaining ingredients. Simmer over a low heat until thick and dark, stirring often to prevent the paste catching on the bottom. Transfer to a clean jar and refrigerate until needed.

Red Curry Paste

Makes 2 cups

Red is the most versatile of Thai curry pastes, used in fish cakes, satays, marinades, stir-fries, as well as curries. A red curry paste is usually made from dried red chillies, rather than fresh ones. This paste keeps for 2–3 weeks in a tightly sealed glass jar in the refrigerator, or store in the freezer for up to 6 months in ice cube trays and thaw cubes as required.

15 dried red chillies, soaked in hot water until soft, about 10 minutes, then drained and chopped finely
2 teaspoons coriander (cilantro) seeds
1 teaspoon cumin seeds
½ teaspoon mace
2 teaspoons white peppercorns
2 small red shallots, peeled

12 cloves garlic, peeled
2 stalks lemongrass, finely sliced
1 tablespoon galangal, chopped
2 tablespoons coriander (cilantro) root, chopped
1 tablespoon lime zest
2 teaspoons salt
2 teaspoons shrimp paste, roasted (see page 24)

Combine coriander seeds, cumin and mace in a small frying pan and toast over a moderate heat until aromatic—this will take about 3 minutes. Grind this mixture with the white peppercorns in a mortar with a pestle. Add remaining ingredients and pound until you have obtained a smooth paste.

Green Curry Paste

Makes 2 cups

Green can be one of the hottest Thai curry pastes. The bite comes from using thin, finger-length green chillies and white peppercorns. This paste keeps for 2–3 weeks in a tightly sealed glass jar in the refrigerator, or store in the freezer for up to 6 months in ice cube trays and thaw cubes as required.

15 green chillies, seeded (pitted) and chopped (adjust the number of chillies to suit your chilli tolerance)
20 white peppercorns, finely ground
2 tablespoons coriander (cilantro) seeds
1 teaspoon cumin seeds
½ cup golden shallots (or onion), peeled and finely chopped
12 cloves garlic, peeled and chopped
4 tablespoons lemongrass, finely sliced
2 teaspoons galangal, chopped
4 teaspoons coriander (cilantro) root, chopped
2 teaspoons lime zest, chopped
2 teaspoons salt
4 teaspoons shrimp paste, roasted (see page 24)

Combine coriander and cumin seeds in a small frying pan and toast over a moderate heat until aromatic—this will take about 3 minutes. Grind these spices and the peppercorns together in a mortar and pestle or spice grinder. Add remaining ingredients and pound until you have obtained a smooth paste.

Yellow Paste

Makes 2 cups

One of the milder Thai pastes, the spices—cardamom, cumin, cloves, nutmeg, cinnamon and fennel—are all indicative of the strong Indian influence on Thai cuisine. This paste keeps for 2–3 weeks in a tightly sealed glass jar in the refrigerator, or store in the freezer for up to 6 months in ice cube trays and thaw the cubes as required.

10 dried red chillies, seeded (pitted), soaked in water for 10 minutes and then finely chopped
3 teaspoons coriander (cilantro) seeds
1½ teaspoons whole cumin seeds
½ teaspoon roasted cardamom seeds
1 teaspoon white peppercorns, ground
1 tablespoon roasted shrimp paste (see page 24)

3 stalks lemongrass, lower stalks finely sliced
12 cloves garlic, peeled and chopped
1 cup golden shallots (or onion), chopped
1 tablespoon galangal, chopped
2 tablespoons coriander (cilantro) root and stem, chopped
2 tablespoons curry powder

Combine coriander, cumin and cardamom seeds in a small frying pan and toast over a moderate heat until aromatic—this will take about 3 minutes. Grind these spices and the peppercorns together in a mortar and pestle or spice grinder. Add remaining ingredients and pound to a smooth paste.

Massaman Paste

Makes 2 cups

Though one of the best known and loved of Thai curries, Massaman is a fairly recent addition to the cuisine. Its exotic perfume comes from sweet fragrant spices such as cloves, cardamom and cassia. Thought to have evolved from an early Persian influence, Massaman has taken on distinctive Thai characteristics. The name literally means 'Muslim man', and the paste is mostly used to make beef or chicken curries, though other meats, such as lamb, can be used. Store in a screw top jar for 2–3 weeks, or freeze in cubes and thaw cubes as required. Keeps for 6 months frozen.

Spice Mixture
2 tablespoons coriander (cilantro) seeds
1 tablespoon cumin seeds
4cm (1½ in) piece cassia
8 cloves
5 cardamom pods
½ teaspoon white pepper
½ teaspoon mace

Paste
12 large dried red chillies, seeded (pitted) and soaked in hot water until soft then drained and finely chopped
12 cloves garlic, peeled
½ cup golden shallots (or onion), peeled and chopped
2 teaspoons galangal, peeled and chopped
2 stalks of lemongrass, trimmed and chopped
3 tablespoons coriander (cilantro) root, washed and chopped
1 teaspoon salt

To make spice mixture: Dry-roast the coriander seeds, cumin seeds, cassia, cloves and cardamom pods in a frying pan over a gentle heat until they begin to colour and smell toasted—about 3 minutes. Place in a mortar and pestle or spice mill with the white pepper and grind to a powder. Stir in the mace.

To make paste: Place the paste ingredients in a mortar and pound to a paste. Mix the spices through the paste.

Essential Spices

Indian, Arab and Chinese merchants, followed by European traders in the 16th century, sailed up the Chao Phraya River to the ancient capital of Ayutthaya which became the centre of the Thai spice trade for hundreds of years. Before chillies were introduced to Asia, the most important hot spice in Thai cooking was pepper—and it's still the most essential spice.

Cassia Bark

A native of China, cassia is one of the ingredients of Chinese five-spice powder. It is related to cinnamon, but is stronger in flavour, and is sold in rolled bark quills or ground into powder. Store in an airtight container.

Coriander (Cilantro) Seeds

Every part of the coriander plant is used in Thai cooking—leaf, stem, root and especially the seeds which are a vital ingredient in most curry pastes. Like many spices, coriander seeds need to be roasted before grinding to release their delicate citrus flavour. Don't buy ground coriander— it can be quite musty. It is far preferable to grind the seeds as required.

Cumin Seeds

Cumin seeds are the fruits of a small herb related to the coriander (cilantro) family. They have a slight licorice, lemon/ginger taste and a distinct aroma. The seeds can be used whole, or roasted and ground for maximum flavour. Cumin seeds are used in curries and as a garnish for salads.

Fennel Seeds

Fennel is used as a vegetable or herb in Europe, but in Asian cuisine the seeds are utilised. With a strong aniseed flavour, the seed looks very much like cumin seed. Fennel seeds are always included in the spices that make the curry powders of Malaysian, Indian and Indonesian curries. In India, fennel seeds are included in betel leaf chew as a breath sweetener and digestive aid.

Peppercorns

Peppercorns are the berries of a climbing vine which grows wild in the Asian rainforest. Small white flowers form clusters of berries like miniature bunches of grapes which turn from green to red as they ripen.

- Green peppercorns are deliciously mild and piquant and 'pop' in the mouth with flavour. They last only about a week off the vine before turning black. Use in stir-fries and as a garnish in curries, particularly hot and spicy jungle curries. Green peppercorns are often preserved in brine or vinegar.

- Black peppercorns are the unripe green berries that have been picked and left to dry in the sun until dark and shrivelled.

- To produce white pepper, the green peppercorns are left on the vine to turn red, then dried and placed in hessian sacks and soaked in water. The black outer skin is then removed. That's why white pepper is more expensive, as it takes longer to grow and more time to process.

Star Anise

A star-shaped pod from the flower of a north Vietnamese tree, star anise has a similar flavour to aniseed or licorice. It is always used in Vietnamese 'Pho' broths or recipes requiring long simmering.

Szechuan Peppercorns

One of the ingredients of Chinese five-spice powder, these are not really a true pepper but are the seed casings of the berries of the Prickly Ash which grows wild in China. They have a peculiar numbing effect on the tongue and are indispensable in Chinese cooking. Buy them whole and store in airtight containers.

Tangerine Peel

From Southern China. Packets of the dried peel can be bought in Asian food stores or supermarkets. With its citrus flavour, tangerine peel is added to braised dishes, or is softened by soaking in hot water, finely chopped and added to stir-fries or noodles as a garnish.

Essential Sauces

Store all these bottles in a dark cupboard or pantry and seal lids tightly after each use. Shelf life is usually 12 months. Oyster sauce should be stored in the refrigerator after opening.

Dark Soy Sauce

Dark soy is fermented longer than light soy sauce and has a thicker texture with a richer flavour. It clings to food and colours it as well.

Fish Sauce

Fish sauce is made by fermenting anchovies in barrels packed with salt. It provides the salty taste in Thai food and helps to balance the other main flavours of sweet, sour and hot. It is used in nearly every Thai dish, much like salt is used in western cooking. The ancient Romans made a similar sauce. A bottle of fish sauce, tightly sealed, keeps for many months. There are various grades of fish sauce; choose a top 'table' variety.

Hoisin Sauce

One of the most popular soy bean sauces, Hoisin sauce has a lovely balance of sweetness, saltiness, garlic and five-spice powder.

Kecap Manis

This sweet soy sauce is an Indonesian staple. The sauce is very thick, perfumed with cassia bark and thickened with palm sugar. Kecap manis is predominantly used in dipping sauces and marinades. Kecap is a Malaysian word from which we have adapted 'ketchup'.

Light Soy Sauce

Soy sauce is made from fermented soy beans and wheat. Light soy sauce is commonly used in Japanese soups and stews. It is saltier than dark soy and is often used in stir-fries and marinades.

Pastes and Sauces: Tamarind, top left, Shrimp Paste, top right, Yellow Bean Sauce, bottom left, Roasted Chilli Paste, bottom right. **Left to right:** Light Soy Sauce, Shaoxing Wine, Sweet Soy Sauce (kecap manis), Rice Vinegar, Dark Soy Sauce.

Oyster Sauce

A rich sauce made from ground oysters that have been boiled, dried, then blended with soy sauce and cooked into a thick sauce. It is a highly prized seasoning, for its distinctive taste and colour, and is commonly used in marinades or stir-fried vegetable dishes.

Sweet Chilli Dipping Sauce

Makes about 3 cups

This would have to be one of the most popular sauces to hit our shores since tomato sauce. If I ask the cooking class who doesn't have this in their pantry, rarely does a hand go up. Often the assumption is that this sauce automatically makes a dish Thai. Strictly speaking, in Thailand sweet chilli sauce is only used with deep-fried or barbecued (grilled) food. It's certainly rarely, if ever, used as a stir-fry sauce or salad dressing ... and never with cream cheese!

We are not bound by tradition and if you like sweet chilli on scrambled eggs, why not? Makes your stir-fry taste good? Then use it. There are heaps of brands on the market but it's so simple to make and tastes better than the commercial variety. It also keeps for months in the fridge, so make a big batch and slurp away to your heart's content.

4–6 large red chillies, chopped
4 cloves garlic, peeled
2 coriander (cilantro) roots, washed, scraped and chopped
1–2 teaspoons salt
2 cups (500g/1 lb) white sugar
1 cup (250ml/8 fl oz) rice or coconut vinegar
1 cup (250ml/8 fl oz) water

Pound the chillies, garlic, coriander root and salt to a paste in a mortar and pestle.

Place the sugar, vinegar and water in a saucepan and bring to the boil and keep boiling until reduced by about a quarter of its original volume. Add the chilli paste and simmer for 5 more minutes. Remove from heat and cool in pot. Transfer to a clean bottle or jar and refrigerate until needed.

Yellow Bean Sauce

There are many sauces made from fermented soy beans. This yellow-brown sauce has a salty, savoury, nutty flavour and is used extensively as a seasoning in stir-fries and soups. Sometimes labelled 'fermented soy bean' or 'soy bean paste'.

Essential Dry Goods

With this selection of ingredients at hand in your pantry you can cook any of our recipes.

Coconut Milk/Cream

Coconut milk is extracted from the grated flesh of mature coconuts which contains the oil so necessary for cooking. (Don't confuse coconut milk with the clear, sweet juice from the shell of green coconuts which is sold as a delightful thirst quencher.) Once opened, canned coconut milk has a very short refrigerated life—no more than 1–2 days. A good storage idea is to pour unused coconut milk into ice cube trays and freeze.

FAQ: What's the difference between coconut milk and coconut cream?

When it comes to buying a tin of coconut milk or cream, find a brand that doesn't have emulsifiers or stabilisers, so that you can separate the milk from the cream. Generally, the milk is used for curry sauces, soups and dressings, while the cream is used to enrich a dish at the finish or to start a curry dish by cracking the cream.

How are they made?

To make your own coconut milk/cream, first crack open a coconut, prise the flesh from the shell, remove the brown skin, grate the flesh and cover with boiling water. Allow to cool, then squeeze through a clean cloth. Let sit for about 15 minutes. The cream will rise to the top and the thinner liquid, or milk, collects underneath. A second pressing is then done which yields less cream and a thinner milk. The cream rises to the top because of its higher fat content, just like cows' milk and cream. Before we homogenised milk, the milk bottle came with a plug of cream on top because the cream had risen. Of course, you could always just buy a tin!

Coconut Vinegar

Coconut vinegar or palm vinegar is cloudy in appearance and has its own unique smoky coconut flavour. Made from the sap of the coconut palm, it is less acid than ordinary vinegar.

FAQ: What's the best vinegar to use?

Several types of vinegars are used in Thai cooking. My favourite is coconut vinegar which has low acidity and is great for making vegetable pickles, sweet chilli or other dipping sauces. It is often sold as palm vinegar. If unavailable, use rice vinegar or just plain old distilled white vinegar. Avoid wine vinegar as its flavour is incompatible with Thai flavours. In Chinese-influenced dishes, black vinegar is used which tastes similar to balsamic vinegar, while red vinegar made from rice is a favourite for seafood and dumplings.

Dried Asian Fungi

Also known as Black Fungus, Cloud Ear or Mouse Ear, these fungi grow on mango and kapok trees, found throughout Asia, China and Japan. Mostly sold in dried form, thy should be stored in an airtight container, and reconstituted by soaking in warm water until soft, about 15 minutes. They will swell to many times their dried size. Then rinse and trim off any woody parts.

Wood fungi add a crunchy texture to stir-fries, soups or salads. Although rather flavourless, the fungi absorb the flavours of the seasonings or sauces in which they are cooked.

Dried Red Chillies

Packets of dried red chillies in the pantry offer a ready chilli supply in an emergency, or if fresh chillies are unavailable. Some Thai recipes, like red curry paste, call for dried red chillies rather than fresh. Soak dried chillies in hot water for about 10 minutes until softened, drain off the water and use the chillies as directed.

Dried Shrimp

Used as a flavouring agent in stir-fries, and available in packets from supermarkets. Only buy those that are deep pink in colour and that 'give' slightly when pressed. Don't buy any that are very hard or smell strongly of ammonia. Store in a sealed container in the refrigerator after opening.

Glass Noodles (Rice Vermicelli)

Made from mung beans and extensively used in vegetarian cooking, these noodles are also known as vermicelli because they are nearly transparent when cooked. Glass noodles are sold dried in tight bundles tied with white cotton; when dry, they are extremely tough and difficult to break. Store as you would pasta.

Eaten in soups, deep-fried into crispy cakes with meat, seafood and seasonings, steamed or served cold in salads, they need to be soaked before using. To use, just place them in a bowl, pour on boiling water, and soak for about 8 minutes or until soft.

Jasmine Rice

Jasmine rice, the favourite Thai rice, is long-grained with a delightfully delicate scent. Long-grain rice has a lower starch content than short-grain rice; the grains are polished, hulled and remain firm, fluffy and separate when cooked. Jasmine rice reheats well.

Oils

All oils are very energy dense which is a polite way of saying they are full of kilojoules, and all should be used with discretion. The way oils are marketed causes much confusion for people. Extra virgin olive oil has been cold-pressed, which means it's not processed, has a stronger flavour and will burn at a lower temperature, leaving a bitter taste. In terms of calories, it has the same as all other oils. Keep in mind that fats and oils are 'flavour carriers'. That's why chicken thigh meat, with its higher fat content, is much more flavoursome than chicken breast.

These days in Thailand most people use blended vegetable oil. Traditional households may still use either rendered pork fat or coconut oil—neither would get the Heart Foundation tick of approval! A far greater quantity of oil is used in Asian cooking, so the finished dish will often have a layer of oil floating on the surface. As the food is prepared by housewives early in the day, the oil forms a seal over the food until the family is ready to eat later that evening.

These are the most suitable oils for Thai cooking:

- Canola oil is low in saturated fats and contains Omega-3 fatty acids; canola is made from rape seeds.

- Coconut oil is pressed from copra (dried coconut meat) and is used for frying and for the manufacture of processed products such as candies, margarine, soaps and cosmetics.

- Corn oil is odourless and almost tasteless. Corn oil has a high smoke point, making it suitable for frying. Also used in baking and salad dressings.

- Peanut oil is especially prized for frying due to its high smoke point. Most American peanut oils are mild in flavour, whereas Chinese peanut oils have a distinctive peanut flavour.

- Safflower and sunflower oil are both pale yellow with a delicate flavour. They are very high in polyunsaturated fats and low in saturated fats. Though they have a relatively low smoke point, both oils are used in cooking as well as for salad dressings.

- Sesame oil is a common ingredient in oriental recipes. The rich, nutty flavour is suitable for use in salad dressings, meat and vegetable dishes. Sesame oil is strongly flavoured and, like extra virgin olive oil, is often used for flavouring. If you like the delicious flavour of sesame oil, it would be better to add a few drops at the end of cooking, rather than risk overheating the oil. Use sparingly.

- Soybean oil is extracted from soy beans and is light yellow in colour. Soybean oil has always been popular as a cooking oil in Chinese cuisine as it is inexpensive, healthy and has a high smoke point.

FAQ: Which oil is best to use?

Without fail, the most commonly asked question in our cooking class is, 'What sort of oil do you use?' When the chef answers that for all-purpose cooking a flavourless vegetable oil, like sunflower or safflower, is preferable, someone usually says in a surprised tone, 'Oh, why not olive oil?' Olive oil has never been used in Asian cooking and its strong, distinctive flavour is not suitable for Asian cooking. Though wonderful for Mediterranean cooking, for a healthy oil, sunflower, safflower or peanut oils are just as good. If you are still hell-bent on using olive oil, use the light variety, which means a lighter flavour, not less fat.

Palm Sugar

Palm sugar is processed from palm tree sap. The sap flows from the tapped palm for 4–6 months, then is boiled down in large vats until it obtains a thick consistency like fudge or caramel. Traditionally it was packed into bamboo tubes or halved coconut shells, but these days it's packed in jars or packets.

Palm sugar comes in a solid lump, so with your knife, shave the sides of the sugar block, then chop the shavings. If you find your palm sugar is very hard it can be pounded easily in a mortar with a pestle, or place it for about 30 seconds in the microwave and it will become soft and easy to chop.

Add it to dressings and sauces to bring out the flavours and adjust the balance of salt and sour. Like sugar, palm sugar keeps for ages and is best stored in an airtight container.

White sugar is also used in Thai cooking, but being native to the Caribbean, was introduced by traders and was considered a sign of wealth, as it was far more expensive than locally processed palm sugar. Now white sugar is readily available in Thailand and is an acceptable substitute in these recipes. The juice pressed from fresh sugar cane is enjoyed throughout South-East Asia.

FAQ: What's the difference between light and dark palm sugar?

Like sugar made from sugar cane, the colour of palm sugar indicates flavour, and can vary from cream to almost black. The pale sugar is lovely and creamy, golden brown palm sugar has a delicious fudge-like flavour, while the very dark palm sugar has a molasses-like bitterness. Some palm sugar is sold as a soft syrup and is referred to as palm honey.

Peanuts

Peanuts grow underground and are actually a member of the legume family rather than a true nut. They are extensively used in Asian cuisine as a source of oil, and to add 'crunch' as a garnish. Because they do not burn at high temperatures, they are great added to stir-fries and form the basis of satay sauce and Indonesian gado gado. To cook raw peanuts, deep-fry in vegetable oil in a wok on low heat for about 10 minutes. Drain on paper towel.

Pickled Galangal

Buy pickled galangal in jars from the supermarket. Related to ginger and turmeric, galangal doesn't taste anything like ginger, having its own unique flavour which can be quite hot. Don't substitute ginger for galangal as this will dramatically alter the final flavours in the dish.

Pickled Garlic

Garlic, pickled in vinegar, can be found in most Asian supermarkets. It is made from young, green garlic and left in whole bulbs as the pickling makes the skins soft and easy to eat.

3 cups (750ml/26 fl oz) water
6 small bulbs young fresh garlic, unpeeled
1½ cups (350ml/12 fl oz) coconut vinegar
2 cups (500g/1 lb) sugar
1½ tablespoons salt

Bring water to the boil in a saucepan. Add the whole unpeeled garlic bulbs, reduce the heat and simmer for 10 minutes. Drain and set aside. Combine the vinegar, sugar and salt in a small saucepan and bring to the boil for 1 minute, stirring occasionally. Reduce heat and simmer until the pickling solution begins to thicken, about 6–8 minutes. Remove from heat and cool. Place the garlic in a glass jar, cover with pickling solution and seal tightly. Store at room temperature in a cool, dark place for 2 weeks or more before using.

To serve: Remove one bulb and cut it crosswise into thin slices. The paper covering will slip off easily as you slice the garlic.

Pickled Krachai

Sometimes called lesser galangal, krachai is also a member of the ginger family. It adds a subtle spicy flavour, especially to seafood. It is quite aromatic with light brown skin and a yellow interior. It is difficult to buy fresh in Australia, so buy pickled in brine. The brand we recommend is 'Cock', imported from Thailand. Sometimes spelt 'Kachai'.

Rice Noodles

Packages of fresh rice noodles are available in Asian supermarkets. Made from rice flour, these noodles are produced in sheets, then cut at three different widths: the flat noodles are 2–3cm, narrow noodles are 5mm, and the thin noodles are 1–2mm in width. The sheets can also be filled with meat and vegetables and steamed as rice rolls. They will only keep for a few days refrigerated.

For greater convenience, buy dried rice noodles which have a long shelf life. They should just be rinsed and softened in hot water for approximately 5 minutes and then added at the last minute to a soup or stir-fry.

Clockwise from top right: Dried Fish, Dried Shrimp, Red Chinese Dates, Tangerine Peel, Sugars (Dark Palm Sugar, Yellow Rock Sugar and Light Palm Sugar).

Roasted Chilli Powder

This powder adds a distinctive rich, roasted flavour to Larb, Pad Thai and Thai salads. Buy it in packets—or it is very easy to make yourself. In a moderate (180°C/350°F/Gas Mark 4) oven, roast six large dried red chillies for 3–5 minutes. Cool. Grind to a powder in a spice mill or mortar and pestle. Store in an airtight container.

Roasted Rice Powder

Made from sticky rice and used extensively in salads. To roast, place 2 tablespoons sticky rice on a shallow baking tray and cook in a preheated 190°C (375°F) oven for 15–20 minutes until golden. Grind in mortar to a fine powder. It is also available in packets from Asian supermarkets.

Shaoxing Rice Wine

Chinese rice wine is also called 'Shaoxing' as it is traditionally made in a city of that name south of Shanghai. It is a fermented sherry-like wine made from glutinous rice and mineral-rich water from Lake Jiang. The wine is allowed to ferment in huge pottery jars which are covered with lotus leaves, sealed with ceramic covers, then covered in mud and allowed to age, sometimes up to ten years. It has a lovely amber colour with a rich, slightly sweetish flavour. Substitute with dry sherry if unavailable. Do not confuse Chinese rice wine with Mirin which is a golden, sweet rice wine from Japan.

Shrimp Paste

This jar of vile-smelling paste is a staple ingredient in most curry pastes. Fermented from tiny, salted shrimp, store it in an airtight container or visitors will think something has crawled into your refrigerator and died! How long does it keep? Months probably, but who would know if it's off?

When making curry pastes, shrimp paste is invariably roasted with the other spices. Wrap in foil and place in a moderate (180°C /350°F/Gas Mark 4) oven for 5–10 minutes. You will know it's ready when you can smell it and the paste crumbles to touch.

Spring Roll Wrappers

Packets of wrappers are available frozen in supermarkets. These light pastry sheets are always square but can be packaged in different sizes: 250, 215 and 125mm square. Thaw until you can peel off as many sheets as required, then wrap and re-freeze the unused sheets. Spring roll wrappers are perfect for any deep-fried food.

Sticky Rice

Often the mention of sticky rice brings to mind one of the best known Thai sweets—sticky rice with coconut cream and mango. However, sticky rice is much more than just a 'dessert' rice. It is the staple rice for Thais from the north, north-east and also their neighbours in Laos. One of the reasons is that this short-grain, glutinous rice variety is more suited to the drier climate of these regions and ensures a more regular crop. When eaten, it is a much heavier, more filling rice and for people from the poorer regions this is very important. Sticky rice is eaten by rolling a small ball in your fingers and then dipping it into a spicy sauce.

Tamarind

Tamarind fruit is the pulp contained in a brown, bean-like pod of the tamarind tree. The sweet-sour flavour is the basis of a multitude of dishes and is used to give the sour flavour to curries.

The best way to use it is fresh (and it does grow throughout Queensland), but the most practical way is to buy a block from the supermarket. If it's fresh it will be soft and pliable. Avoid any that's hard or leathery. Buy tamarind puree or blocks of tamarind pulp, wrap in cling wrap and store the block in your refrigerator. It keeps for months.

FAQ: How do I make tamarind water?

Take about 1 tablespoon of tamarind pulp and place in a bowl, pour about half a cup of hot water over the pulp. When the water is cool, mash the pulp with a fork, then push it through a sieve, collecting the thick water in a bowl. If it's too thick, just dilute with some water. Discard the seeds and fibre. The tamarind water should be slightly thick, like cream. Tamarind concentrate is a useful substitute, but the result from using the pulp is worth the few extra minutes it takes to make.

Yellow Rock Sugar

This is a compound of white sugar, brown sugar and honey. Used primarily in Chinese master stock, pickles, teas and red braising, it is available in boxes and resembles small translucent amber rocks. Store the same as you would sugar.

Essential Fresh Ingredients

As with all cooking, the success of Thai food is entirely dependent on the freshness of the ingredients. Just as you shop each week for staples like potatoes and onions, or herbs like parsley, so there are essential Thai fresh ingredients which should be included in your weekly shopping list.

This list is not long—garlic, golden shallots, chillies, ginger, limes, galangal, coriander (cilantro), Thai basil, lemongrass, kaffir lime leaves and mint. Readily available in supermarkets, much of this Asian produce can be grown in home gardens in warm temperate through to tropical climates.

Our chef Annette's hobby is her rambling home garden, a profusion of palms and tropical succulents including heliconias, frangipani and hibiscus nestled around the swimming pool. But also thriving in her lush garden is a continuous supply of fresh Thai essentials: coriander, Thai basil, lemongrass and chillies; trees of kaffir lime, papaya, candlenut and banana; while cha plu vines creep below the shaded canopy providing an edible ground cover. Thick clumps of scented broad leaf galangal, ginger, turmeric and cardamom add to her garden display. In late summer, the turmeric produces such a delicately beautiful white flower that it makes this rhizome worth growing for the bloom alone.

Annette's self-sufficient garden is an inspiring example of Asian fresh ingredients contributing to the beauty of her subtropical landscape—and all nestled around a suburban house.

With the following fresh ingredients on hand, plus the essential Thai sauces, pastes and spices in your pantry and refrigerator, all that remains is to buy some fresh meat or seafood and you're ready to heat up your wok.

Chillies

Chillies were introduced into Asia by the Portuguese in the 1600s. There are hundreds of varieties of chillies and they are used not just for their spicy heat, but also for flavour. Chilli connoisseurs talk about the different notes and flavours like a wine lover talks about wine. The small birdseye chillies are the hottest.

Chillies have many effects on the body—helping to clear nasal passages, aid the digestive process, stimulate the sweat glands which lowers the body temperature, and generally create a feeling of wellbeing.

The heat from chillies varies tremendously, depending on the variety and on factors such as the growing environment—chillies on the sunniest side of the bush are always hotter than those on the shaded side. Any climatic condition that causes stress in the plant will increase the level of heat in the pods.

The heat in chillies is contained in the alkaloid capsaicin oil and is very difficult to remove from the skin or palate. If cutting hot chillies, wear thin rubber gloves to avoid the burn. Failing that, do what they do in the emergency ward of hospitals when people have been sprayed with pepper spray, and coat the burning patch of skin with Mylanta liquid.

To test the level of heat of your chillies, cut off the top, run your finger across the cut edge, then rub your finger on your tongue and wait for the result! The hottest part of the chilli is the white inner membrane. If you only want a mild dish, leave out the seeds and membrane, using only the outer coloured flesh.

If the heat in a spicy meal is too much for you, the best way to neutralise the burn is to eat a teaspoon of sugar; the sugar will neutralise the alkaloid. Contrary to what most men say, beer does not work! Milk or yoghurt will also reduce the discomfort as the fat in these will cling to the capsaicin oil and help disperse it.

Unfortunately, if you make your dish too hot there really is no way to reduce the heat apart from starting again. Instead, bluff your way through it, nonchalantly telling everyone it's a little recipe you picked up on your last trip to Thailand and it's meant to be really hot.

To grow chillies
When you find the chillies you like, they can be a great source of planting stock. Simply cut the fruit open, scrape out the seeds and wash in water. Allow the seeds to dry, then plant in full sun in enriched soil around the garden or in pots. The chillies can be picked green or left to ripen to a rich red colour. Chilli plants are short-lived perennials so you will need to replant every couple of years. If you live in a very cold area, chillies will go dormant over the winter, but will generally start producing again during the spring.

FAQ: Red and green chillies—what's the difference?
The difference between red and green chillies is simply that green chillies are under-ripe and red chillies are mature. Flavour-wise, it's similar to the difference between red and green capsicum (sweet pepper). The red chillies have more sugar so are sweeter, and the green are more herbaceous in flavour.

FAQ: Do I eat the chilli seeds and membranes?
Whether you de-seed or not depends on how hot you want your chilli and what you are going to do with it. If I want to make a lovely garnish of chilli strips, obviously I remove the seeds. If I am making a paste using large chillies, I often remove the seeds so my paste is smooth and not full of hard woody seeds. So that the heat is not too insipid, I will throw in a handful of little birdseye chillies with their seeds to add some bite.

Coriander (cilantro)

A relative of the carrot, coriander leaves, root and stem are all used in Thai cooking. With your knife, scrape off the outer skin of the root before chopping it together with the stems. Don't cook coriander leaves—they will go black and add bitterness to the dish. Just add the leaves as a garnish to a stir-fry, curry or salad.

Refrigerate fresh bunches of coriander wrapped lightly in a damp tea towel.

To grow coriander
Coriander seedlings will not transplant, so sow the seeds straight into sunny, well-drained garden beds or pots. Best grown in the cooler weather, coriander 'bolts' or goes to seed very rapidly in the extreme heat.

Galangal

Related to ginger and turmeric, fresh galangal rhizomes are appearing more frequently in Australian supermarkets. Just peel the rhizomes and then slice and store in a sealed bag in the freezer, as with ginger.

The name is derived from an Arabic word, khalanjan, which means 'Chinese ginger'. Native to South-East Asia, galangal was used in Europe in the Middle Ages as a medicine as well as a spice.

Galangal provides a distinctive sharp, aromatic taste, more like mustard than ginger, and is most easily recognised in Thai soups. There are two types of galangal: greater galangal and lesser galangal, which is also known as krachai. The smaller growing krachai has exquisitely perfumed white flowers, while the greater galangal produces spikes of small, unperfumed blooms.

To grow galangal

Plant only in subtropical and tropical regions, as galangal can't tolerate frost. Buy fresh small rhizomes from the supermarket and plant in the spring. It requires moist, well-drained, enriched soil and plenty of space, as the plants can reach over 2 metres. The plant has long, dark green, spear-shaped leaves and the flowers strongly resemble irises.

Garlic

Used in practically every Thai recipe, garlic is highly nutritious, easy to buy, grow and store. When crushing garlic, break up the bulb into cloves. Place the flat side of your kitchen knife on each clove of garlic, bang down with the palm of your hand, and the skin should just slip off. Once the skin is removed, bang down again with the side of the knife to crush the clove. Then chop finely or pound in a mortar with a pestle.

If deep-frying garlic, slice the cloves lengthways and cook until a nutty, light brown colour. Do not overcook or it will taste very acrid. Deep-fried garlic (and golden shallots) are wonderful sprinkled on top of salads, giving a lovely crunchy texture to the garnish.

To grow garlic

In early autumn, push loosened garlic bulbs into light, well-drained soil in a sunny position, with the tops just below the surface. Mulch well and water regularly until the tops turn brown. Harvest in about 6 months, before the tops have completely died back. Dry the whole bulbs on racks or by hanging for 2–3 weeks until the skins become papery. Good air circulation is vital.

Note: Do not plant imported garlic bulbs which could introduce virus diseases to your soil.

Ginger

Fresh ginger is absolutely essential to Thai cooking. Very young rhizomes, known as stem ginger or green ginger, are peeled and eaten raw in salads, added to stir-fries and curries, pickled or cooked in syrup. Young, slightly spicy shoots can be used as a vegetable.

Don't buy ginger rhizomes if the skin is dark and withered, as they will be long past their use-by date. Choose firm-skinned pieces and peel them thinly, as the flesh nearest the skin has the most flavour. The easiest way to peel ginger is to scrape the skin off with the edge of a soup spoon. Store peeled, sliced ginger in a plastic bag in the freezer or for 3–4 weeks in an airtight container in the refrigerator.

To grow ginger

Buy fresh, small rhizomes from the supermarket and plant in the spring, in a well-drained, nutrient-enriched soil. The

plants, which grow to about one metre tall with thin, strap-like leaves, die down in the cooler months, but any unharvested rhizomes will emerge the following season. To harvest, simply slice off a section of underground rhizome, leaving the remainder of the plant to continue growing.

Golden Shallots

Australians commonly but mistakenly refer to spring onions as a shallot. Shallots are in fact a small bulb with a superb, delicate flavour. The base of the shallot is composed of about twelve onions lightly attached to each other. The leaves are tubular like an onion's, but shorter and thinner. The Asian shallot has a purplish skin with a pinkish interior. Shallots are long-keeping and will store for up to 12 months in a dry place. Golden shallots make a wonderful crunchy garnish for salads, soups and stir-fries. These can be found in packets down the Asian aisle of your local supermarket and are a reasonable substitute if time is limited. If you do have the time or inclination, the homemade version is far superior.

Crispy Golden Shallots
1 cup (250ml/8 fl oz) vegetable oil such as sunflower, peanut or safflower
4–6 golden shallots, peeled and thinly sliced

Heat the oil in a wok over moderate heat. If too hot, the shallots will burn too quickly and become bitter. Add the shallots and cook, stirring occasionally until golden brown. This may take up to 10 minutes. Remove with a slotted spoon and drain well on paper towel. Best to use within the day. When the oil is cool, strain through a sieve and transfer to a clean jar. The oil will be infused with a delicious nutty shallot flavour and can be used for cooking vegetables, noodles or fried rice.

To grow golden shallots
Choose a sunny, well-drained position and push the bulbs into organically enriched soil, leaving the tops visible. In subtropical areas, plant in March–April, in cooler climates plant in late winter. A single bulb will multiply into about 6–12 bulbs so don't plant them too close together. Harvest shallots before flowering, when their green tops start to flop over. Store in a dry place, saving the medium-sized bulbs for replanting next season.

Kaffir Limes/Leaves

An indispensable fresh ingredient, this citrus fruit has very little juice; it's the skin and leaves which are highly prized. The knobby skin is zested then added to most curry pastes. Buy fresh leaves from the supermarket and store in a bag in the freezer. Use the leaf in the same way as a bay leaf, adding a leaf to soups, curries or steaming rice to impart a subtle lime scent. To finely slice the leaf, fold it in half along its spine and remove the tough stem. Roll up the leaf from the tip to the stem, and slice into very fine shreds. Add to stir-fries, salads or use as a garnish. The juice is used to enhance dressings and perfume a finished dish.

To grow a kaffir lime tree
This citrus tree is easy to grow in most climates and makes a good pot specimen. The tree requires regular trimming and fertilising as with other citrus varieties. Apply white oil or soap sprays to prevent scale, sooty mould and citrus leaf miner.

Lemongrass

An important aromatic in Asia where the lemon tree will not grow. Buy by the stem or in small bunches in the fresh food section of the supermarket. The whole lemongrass stalk is used for infusing soups or even jasmine rice while it's steaming. The bottom inner core is used for cooking. Peel off the tough outer leaves and finely slice the bottom 15cm of the stem. As the knife gets harder to use, you will know that you have chopped too far up the stem.

To grow lemongrass

Growing in grassy clumps, lemongrass prefers hot, wet summers and dry, warm winters. Trouble-free to grow, it can tolerate frost but dislikes wet feet. In cooler areas, the tops should not be cut until the end of winter as they help to protect the centre of the plant from the cold. Plant in spring in cooler areas and during the wet season in the tropics. With your knife, just cut the stems off close to the root as required.

Mint

Originating in ancient Greece, mint is a commonly used ingredient in Thai salads. Do not keep cut mint stems in water, the leaves will blacken. Do not wash before storing, just store in a plastic bag in the refrigerator and wash and dry prior to use.

To grow mint

There are over 30 varieties of mint, which are easy to grow from seed in moist spots in the garden or in pots.

Thai Basil

Thais love basil, adding it to curries, stir-fries, salads and vegetable dishes. If you can't buy Thai basil, substitute ordinary sweet basil. All basil is related to mint.

To grow Thai basil

As with all basil, it is easy to grow in pots in the warmer months, as basil loves the sun. Thai basil has pointy leaves and purple stems with a strong anise flavour and is very pretty, especially when in flower. Basil will not grow during the cold winter months.

Water Chestnuts

Water chestnuts are nutritious, containing B vitamins, and can be eaten raw or cooked. With their crispy white flesh under a thin brown skin, water chestnuts are used for their crunchy texture and are available tinned or fresh. To prepare fresh water chestnuts, peel or scrub well and slice thinly before adding to stir-fry dishes and soups. Store fresh water chestnuts in the fridge for several weeks; they can also be frozen.

Essential Utensils

Thai cooking is an exercise in minimalism—a wok, a wok shovel to stir the ingredients and a high flame is all that is required to cook most Thai meals. Add a chopping board, chef's knife, mortar and pestle, steamer basket, wok sieve and a rice cooker and you have a fully equipped Thai kitchen.

Knives

A good quality cook's knife (about 16–18cm or 6–7 in long) and a small paring knife will cover all contingencies. Do spend more and buy a reputable brand, as a favourite knife is invaluable and will last a lifetime—a true cook's companion!

There is a vast array of specialised knives and Chinese cleavers which are more than useful, but not essential.

Mortar and Pestle

An absolute 'must have' for the Thai kitchen, a mortar and pestle is the original food processor.

Unequalled for crushing spices and herbs into a paste, the pounding of stone against stone produces a much smoother paste than the tearing action of modern food processor blades. The action of the two stones pounding together breaks down the cell structure, releasing all the juices of the herbs. Let the pestle do the work while your arm provides the rhythm. Annette maintains that she can hold a glass of wine in one hand and pound with the other, while not spilling a drop.

Buy a granite mortar, about 20cm (8 in) in diameter. Any smaller and the food pops out during pounding, any bigger and you'll save on weight-lifting sessions at the gym. Don't buy marble mortars as used by pharmacies; they are unsuitable for kitchen purposes, too light and too small. Often in Asian supermarkets you'll see tall-sided terracotta mortars with long wooden pestles. These are traditionally used for making Thai salads, such as Som Tam. While useful to have, they're not essential.

Leave the mortar permanently on your kitchen bench so that it's available for all those small jobs, like crushing garlic or grinding peppercorns and spices. Glue fabric pads to the bottom of the mortar so that you can slide it around without scratching your bench tops. After use, just wipe it out with a damp cloth.

Rice Cooker

While you can steam rice the traditional way in a tightly lidded saucepan, you can also steam rice like modern Thais—in an electric rice cooker. These indispensable kitchen appliances cook the rice, automatically turn it off when cooked, then keep it warm for several hours.

Steamer Baskets

Steamers are so versatile. Use them to steam vegetables, fish, meats, even custards, or use them to smoke fish or chicken. Available in bamboo or metal, buy several tiers that stack on top of one another. Steamers come in different diameters so ensure that the basket sits just inside the top lip of your wok.

Bamboo steamers are the best for steaming food like dumplings because the woven lids absorb the steam and prevent any condensation dripping onto the dumplings.

Wok

A wok is simply a frypan with high sides. It can be used to cook just about everything—stir-fries, curries, noodles, even omelettes. A wok can steam, smoke, simmer, sizzle and fry. A wok is a one-stop cooking utensil.

The old adage 'you get what you pay for' does not apply when buying a wok. Spurn the fancy, celebrity chef branded woks, ignore expensive Teflon-coated woks, bypass electric woks (they don't generate enough heat) and instead head to your nearest Asian supermarket and buy a cheap, pressed steel wok. The money saved can be spent foolishly on other things, like wine or shoes.

A wok with a 35cm (14 in) diameter will suit most families; any bigger and domestic gas stoves struggle to sufficiently distribute the heat over the entire surface.

Woks can have one long handle or two small ones—it's purely a matter of personal preference. The two-handled wok gives more control when lifting on and off the stove, while professional chefs prefer the long handle so they can tilt, shake and swirl the ingredients during cooking.

Steel woks must first be 'seasoned' to remove the manufacturer's protective coating. Wash in hot soapy water, dry thoroughly, pour about a tablespoon of vegetable oil into the wok, heat over a flame, swirl the oil around all the surfaces, then tip it out. Wipe the oily residue around the wok with a dry paper towel. Repeat the process and it's now ready to use.

After cooking, wash and dry the wok thoroughly, but don't use abrasive scourers which will damage the surface. Never put your wok in a dishwasher. Put the washed wok back on the flame with a little cooking oil and rub the hot oil around the sides with a paper towel. You need to do this after every use to prevent rust. Over time, the steel surface develops a black patina which just requires a simple wipe over after use.

Wok Shovel

Costing just a few dollars, a metal wok shovel or spatula is essential for stirring and turning food during cooking. They come with different length handles; the short-handled ones are more than adequate for home use.

Wok Sieve

A wok sieve is another useful cheap utensil, great for straining or lifting food from hot stock or oil. The sieve is a mesh basket made from silver or brass wire and has a long wooden handle.

FAQ: How long does it take to cook?

Or how long is a piece of string? There are many variables—the sort of oven or stove being used, how much is being cooked and how the individual palate prefers the final taste or texture. Most recipes will try to be reasonably accurate but recipes are meant to guide you, not necessarily be followed to the letter. Sometimes it just takes a bit of practice and with that comes confidence in judging cooking times.

FAQ: It's burning ... what should I do?

My favourite question! Many years ago in a class a student said to me, 'I always burn my garlic, what should I do?' Very simple—turn down the heat. Something's browning too quickly in the oven? Turn down the heat. Ingredients with a high natural sugar content like garlic, onions, or those with lots of oil like nuts or shredded coconut, will colour very quickly—again, simply turn down the heat.

Starters and Snacks

Thais love to snack. Often only one main meal is eaten each day, the rest of the day's menu is filled with small snacks from different street vendors. Bangkok streets can look more like food markets than main thoroughfares! Some of the vendors have mobile carts that roam all over the place. In Thailand, most food is eaten outside the house and comes under the broad term of street food. If you are interested in savouring the best of Thai food, it is essential to eat from the streets. The variety is much more infinite than that found on restaurant menus.

I am often asked, 'Aren't you afraid of getting sick?' My feeling is that if this is a concern, I may as well stay home. In my decades of travelling throughout Asia, the rare times I have been sick have always occurred after eating in restaurants or in tourist cafes. A street food vendor's livelihood depends on a quick turnover of well-cooked food, with a decent hygiene standard. They certainly don't want to jeopardise their only source of income by offending regular customers.

In a traditional Thai meal, there is no such thing as an entree, as there are no divisions between courses. All dishes are shared and eaten with rice. Thai restaurants catering to European tourists adapt their menu to suit the clientele, so you will find the list of dishes that make up the entree selection are usually taken from the traditional snacks found outside on the street stalls. So if you are travelling in Thailand and are in the mood for dishes like fish cakes, spring rolls, satays and curry puffs, the best place to find them is where all the locals eat—and that's out and about at food markets and from street vendor carts.

The following selection of dishes has been inspired by the myriad snacks and appetisers that I've enjoyed on my travels. Some are quite traditional, while others have been given a modern twist. —A.F.

Steamed Prawn and Chicken Dumplings

Makes about 35

A popular street side snack, these dumplings are a wonderful starter for a Thai-style meal or just as a snack with drinks. They are accented with three great condiments: Sweet Black Bean Sauce, Si Racha chilli sauce (or any hot sweet chilli sauce) and Golden Fried Garlic (see next page).

250g (8 oz) chicken mince (ground)
250g (8 oz) green prawn meat, finely chopped
2 green spring onions, including some of the green top, finely chopped
1 cup water chestnuts, finely chopped
4 cloves garlic, crushed with a pinch of salt in a mortar with a pestle

1 egg
2 tablespoons fish sauce
1 tablespoon oyster sauce
1 teaspoon ground white pepper
1 tablespoon light palm sugar
1 packet wonton wrappers
1 egg, beaten and mixed with a tablespoon of water

Mix all ingredients together until well combined. Fill wontons with about 1 dessertspoon of mix. Brush edges of wonton with a little egg wash and close the sides.

Fill a large wok half full of water and bring to the boil. Place wontons in a bamboo steamer basket and then place the basket in the wok over boiling water. Cover and cook for about 10–15 minutes, then transfer to serving platter.

To serve, spoon a little Golden Fried Garlic with its oil over the wontons, then a drizzle of Sweet Black Bean Sauce and some Si Racha chilli sauce to taste.

Si Racha Sauce

A sweet hot sauce that comes from the seaside port of Si Racha, but any hot sweet chilli sauce would work with these dumplings. Buy Si Racha sauce in Asian supermarkets.

Sweet Black Bean Sauce

½ cup (125ml/4 fl oz) sweet soy sauce (kecap manis)
¼ cup (60ml/2 fl oz) coconut vinegar
¼ cup (60g/2 oz) dark palm sugar

Combine all ingredients in a small pan and bring to the boil. Stir until sugar dissolves. Remove from heat. Keeps for weeks in the refrigerator. Best warmed slightly before serving.

Golden Fried Garlic

Used frequently to garnish all sorts of dishes. It does require a bit of care, because if the oil is too hot, the garlic becomes bitter and acrid. So don't overheat the oil and remove garlic when it's just starting to turn pale golden.

½ cup (125ml/4 fl oz) vegetable oil
10 cloves garlic, sliced thinly and evenly

Heat oil to moderate and fry garlic until it's aromatic and pale golden, about 2 minutes. Remove from heat, stirring as the pan cools. Refrigerate until needed. Keeps about 1 week in the refrigerator.

Ma Hor of Pork, Prawns and Peanuts

Makes about 24 pieces

The name means 'galloping horses' and this is a wonderful starter to a Thai banquet. Nutty, sweet and salty flavours all contrast with the acidity of the fruit, a perfect foil for the rich topping.

3 tablespoons vegetable oil
150g (5 oz) pork mince (ground)
150g (5 oz) green prawn (shrimp) meat, finely chopped
2 cloves garlic
1 tablespoon coriander (cilantro) root
¼ teaspoon white peppercorns
3 tablespoons fish sauce
5 tablespoons palm sugar

¼ cup roasted unsalted crushed peanuts
¼ cup Crispy Golden Shallots, preferably homemade (see page 29)
12 mandarin or orange segments
12 bite-sized wedges of pineapple, about 1 cm (½ in) thick
½ large red chilli, de-seeded (pitted) and shredded for garnish
handful of coriander (cilantro) leaves for garnish

Heat 1 tablespoon of the oil and fry the pork mince, stirring constantly until cooked. Remove and set aside. Reheat another tablespoon of oil and repeat with the prawns.

Make a paste with the garlic, coriander root and peppercorns. Heat remaining oil and gently fry the paste. Add the fish sauce and palm sugar and simmer gently until thick. Add the pork, prawns, peanuts and Crispy Golden Shallots, stirring to prevent the mixture clumping. Remove from heat and cool.

When ready to serve, place a scant teaspoon of mixture on top of fruit segments and garnish with chilli strips and coriander leaf. Arrange fruit pieces on a platter.

Miang of Spanner Crab, Coconut, Mint and Pomelo

Serves 8

Miang in Thai means 'to wrap' and miang can use lettuce, wild pepper leaves, thin omelette or freshly steamed rice noodles, to name just a few 'wraps'. My first experience of miang was at the Bangkok weekend market, where I came across an old woman who had a selection of ingredients in a large enamel bowl. She made me a very common snack called Miang Cha Plu which refers to the wild pepper leaf used in this variation. After smearing the leaf with a sweet sauce, she added a piece or two of ginger, lime, peanut, chilli, roasted coconut, lemongrass and dried prawns (shrimp). It was all eaten in one bite, giving me my first experience of the Thai rainbow effect, where all the flavours explode at once and you get the amazing interplay of the different ingredients. And to think something this good was just a simple snack!

The cha plu leaf comes from the pepper family and is often referred to as wild betel leaf, being from the same family as the betel leaf used for chewing. These plants are found growing wild and in gardens throughout Asia. The leaves should be available in Asian grocery stores. If unavailable, use baby spinach leaves or soft lettuce.
This recipe is a very glamourised version of the everyday miang, but still uses many of the traditional elements. If the thought of picking over crabmeat is too much (and it must be fresh crab), then use cooked prawns (shrimp).

16 wild pepper leaves
200g (7 oz) fresh crabmeat, picked over to remove traces of shell
2 tablespoons young ginger, peeled and finely shredded
2 tablespoons shredded fresh coconut
¼ cup mint leaves
1 cup pomelo or grapefruit chunks, with all skin and pith removed
2 stalks lemongrass, finely sliced, bottom half only and tough outer leaves removed

4 kaffir lime leaves, shredded into fine slivers
½ red chilli, de-seeded (pitted) and finely shredded
¼ cup coriander (cilantro) leaves

Dressing
1 teaspoon roasted chilli paste (see page 12)
1 teaspoon light palm sugar
1 tablespoon fish sauce
3 tablespoons lime juice
2 tablespoons coconut cream

To make miang: In a bowl, combine the crabmeat, ginger, coconut, mint, pomelo, lemongrass and kaffir lime leaves. Add the dressing and toss gently to combine. Divide the crab between the pepper leaves and garnish with chilli strips and coriander leaves.

To make dressing: Combine all ingredients in a bowl and stir to combine.

Crispy Prawn Wontons Stuffed with Pork and Basil

Serves 8 as part of a selection of dishes

These have been a favourite at the restaurant and cooking school over the years. The pork stuffing is seasoned with classic red curry paste. This dish can be simplified by omitting the stuffing and just wrapping the prawn in a basil leaf and then wrapping it again in the wonton pastry. Like most deep-fried foods, these are best served with a sweet-and-sour style sauce like sweet chilli.

125g (4 oz) pork mince (ground)
1 teaspoon red curry paste (see page 13)
2 kaffir lime leaves, finely shredded
1 teaspoon fish sauce
pinch of white sugar
1 green spring onion, white part only, finely chopped
2 tablespoons coriander (cilantro) leaves and stems, finely chopped

large basil leaves for wrapping
16 large green prawns (shrimp), de-veined, tail on and butterflied
16 square wonton wrappers
1 egg, lightly beaten and mixed with a tablespoon of water
2 cups (500ml/17 fl oz) vegetable oil
Sweet Chilli Dipping Sauce (see page 18)

Combine pork mince, curry paste, lime leaf, fish sauce, sugar, green spring onion and coriander leaves. Mix well. Place the pork mince in a piping bag and pipe 1 teaspoon of mix down the back of each prawn. (If a piping bag is not available, spoon 1 teaspoon of mix down the back of the prawn.) Now wrap 1 basil leaf around the stuffed prawn, and then wrap the prawn in a wonton, leaving the tail protruding. Seal with egg wash.

Heat vegetable oil in wok to medium heat and deep-fry the prawns until the wonton pastry is golden and the prawns cooked through, about 3–5 minutes.

Transfer to a serving plate and serve with sweet chilli dipping sauce.

Moo Grob with Lime and Chilli Jam

Serves 6–8 as part of a selection of dishes

This should come with a caveat: 'Beware, this is wickedly good!' But if you do what the Thais do and only eat this dish occasionally, you won't need to worry too much about having your health insurance up-to-date. Moo Grob is often eaten as a relish to accompany other dishes and would be a wonderful treat as part of your next Thai dinner party.

1 kg (2 lb) pork belly with skin
1 teaspoon salt
1 tablespoon white peppercorns
10 cloves garlic, peeled
3 coriander (cilantro) roots, washed
3 tablespoons soy sauce
3 tablespoons white vinegar
2 tablespoons salt
oil for deep-frying

Lime and Chilli Jam
3 tablespoons roasted chilli paste
1 tablespoon water
1½ tablespoons light palm sugar
3 tablespoons lime juice

Place pork in a pot and cover with water. Add the salt, peppercorns, garlic, coriander roots and soy sauce. Bring to the boil, skim well and simmer until cooked, about 1 hour. Remove pork from stock and cool.

With a sharp knife score the skin well, crosshatching at ½ cm intervals. Rub the skin well with vinegar and salt and leave to dry overnight. Brush off excess salt and cut meat into 2–3cm strips across the grain.

Heat oil in a wok and fry pork until skin is crispy. When cool enough to handle, slice into smaller bite-sized pieces and serve with Lime and Chilli Jam.

To make jam: Combine chilli paste, water and palm sugar in a pan and heat until sugar is dissolved. Remove from heat and stir in lime juice.

Curry Puffs with Chicken and Vegetable

Makes about 24

These delicious little savoury pastries are sold at markets all over Thailand, but the bite-sized traditional version is quite painstaking to make. Although still a little time consuming to prepare, I have simplified the dough and increased the size to make them far more user-friendly. However, if I ever suggested putting them back on the restaurant menu, there would be a kitchen mutiny.

2 teaspoons coriander (cilantro) root
2 cloves garlic, peeled
¼ teaspoon white pepper
1 tablespoon oil
500g (1 lb) minced (ground) chicken
3 tablespoons fish sauce
2 teaspoons light palm sugar
2 tablespoons good quality commercial curry powder
1 medium potato, peeled and finely diced

½ cup coriander (cilantro) leaves, coarsely chopped

Pastry
2 cups plain flour
½ teaspoon salt
75g (2½ oz/¼ cup) butter, melted
¼ cup (60ml/2 fl oz) coconut milk
vegetable oil for deep-frying

To make the filling: Make a paste with the coriander root, garlic and pepper. Heat the oil to moderate and gently fry the paste, then add the chicken, fish sauce, palm sugar and curry powder. Stir until cooked. Add the potato and just a little water to cover, and cook covered for another 10 minutes or until potato is tender. If necessary, cook uncovered for a few minutes to evaporate any liquid. Cool completely and then stir in coriander leaves.

To make pastry: Combine salt and flour in a bowl and stir in butter and coconut milk to make a stiff dough. Transfer to a lightly floured surface and knead lightly until smooth. Wrap in cling wrap and rest for 45 minutes.

Divide pastry into 24 balls and roll out into 10cm circles. Place a tablespoon of cooled filling mixture on pastry and fold over, pressing the edges together to seal. These are always finished with a decorative rope edge which can be a bit tricky to do. Just leave them as is, or to finish traditionally, start at one edge of the pastry and fold about ½ cm of the edge over. Keep folding around the edge, crimping as you go.

To cook: Heat oil in a wok to medium heat and cook until pastry is golden and crisp. Drain on absorbent paper and serve with sweet chilli sauce.

Spicy Pork and Shiitake Mushroom Sausages with Dipping Sauce

Makes 12

One of my favourite snacks from Thai street barbecue (grill) vendors is sausage. There are countless versions throughout Thailand. To make this recipe easier at home, I have omitted the process of forcing the meat into sausage skins. Instead I've just formed the filling into patties to serve with the traditional condiments of herbs, lettuce and dipping sauce. It's still a great result and something easy for your next barbecue.

2 coriander (cilantro) roots, washed
6 cloves garlic, peeled
pinch of salt
8 fresh shiitake mushrooms, stems trimmed and finely chopped
1 tablespoon vegetable oil
600g (21 oz) fatty pork mince (ground)
1 tablespoon light palm sugar
2 tablespoons fish sauce
1 tablespoon soy sauce
1 tablespoon Shaoxing wine
2 teaspoons five-spice powder

1–4 small red chillies, finely chopped
sprigs of coriander (cilantro), mint and basil
1 head of soft lettuce
tamarind dipping sauce

Tamarind Dipping Sauce
2 golden shallots, peeled
6 cloves garlic, peeled
1 cup (250ml/8 fl oz) tamarind water
¼ cup (60ml/2 fl oz) fish sauce
½ cup (125g/4 oz) dark palm sugar
1 tablespoon chilli powder

In a mortar, make a paste with the coriander roots, garlic and salt. Lightly sauté the mushrooms in the vegetable oil until softened. In a large bowl combine the paste, mushrooms, pork, palm sugar, fish sauce, soy sauce, Shaoxing wine, five-spice powder and red chillies. Mix thoroughly and shape into 12 patties.

Barbecue (grill) for about 6–8 minutes, then transfer to serving platter with the sprigs of herbs and lettuce and serve with tamarind dipping sauce.

Note: If you're feeling adventurous, the mixture can be piped into sausage casings which you can buy from your local butcher.

To make dipping sauce: Heat a wok and add the shallots and garlic, stirring until the skins start to blacken in a few places. Pound the fried shallots and garlic to a paste in a mortar. Transfer to a saucepan, add the tamarind water, fish sauce and palm sugar. Stir over a low heat until syrupy. Take off the heat and stir in the chilli powder.

Prawn Cakes with Peanut and Lime Dipping Sauce

Makes about 12

These are a Royal Thai snack and are an up-market version of the ubiquitous fish cake. Like many palace recipes they are based on an everyday dish, but have been given a greater appeal with the use of prawns (shrimp), and would be traditionally served with a very elaborate presentation and a selection of dipping sauces to tantalise the palate.
The texture of these sorts of fritters often surprises Western palates because they are quite bouncy—which is a polite way of saying 'rubbery'. They are meant to be like that, and this comes from stretching the protein strands in either the seafood or meat when it's minced (ground). If you don't want them authentically springy, just don't overwork the seafood or meat in the food processor.

Prawn Cakes
250g (8 oz) good quality fresh fish fillets, chopped finely
2 tablespoons red curry paste (see page 13)
2 tablespoons fish sauce
1 teaspoon rice or corn flour
1 egg
250g (8 oz) green prawn meat, finely chopped
2 spring onions (scallions), finely sliced, including a little of the green part
2 double kaffir lime leaves, centre spine removed and finely chopped
2 cups (500ml/17 fl oz) vegetable oil

Peanut and Lime Dipping Sauce
½ cup (125g/4 oz) caster sugar
¼ cup (60ml/2 fl oz) water
¼ cup (60ml/2 fl oz) lime juice
1 tablespoon fish sauce
1 tablespoon finely diced red chillies, hot or mild as you prefer
½ small Lebanese cucumber, de-seeded (pitted) and finely diced
1 tablespoon roasted unsalted peanuts, finely crushed

To make prawn cakes: Place the fish, curry paste, fish sauce, rice or corn flour and egg in the bowl of a food processor and mix to a rough paste. Don't worry if there is the odd bit of unprocessed fish. Transfer to a bowl and mix in the prawn meat, spring onions and kaffir lime leaves. With wet hands, form the mix into 12 even-sized patties and flatten out to about 1 cm (½ in) thickness.

Heat oil in a wok to a medium heat and fry the prawn cakes in batches until golden. This will take about 4–5 minutes. Drain on paper towel and serve with Lime and Peanut Dipping Sauce.

To make sauce: Combine the sugar and water in a saucepan and simmer until sugar is dissolved. Cool and then stir in the remaining ingredients.

Ning's Fresh Rice Paper Rolls with Pork and Herbs

Makes about 16

These healthy snacks are always associated with Vietnamese cuisine, but I've had many variations throughout South-East Asia. As with many recipes, it's more about understanding the technique and then creating your own version. The common thread is usually a filling of fresh herbs, finely shredded vegetables, lettuce and rice noodles— then you can add your own choice of meat or seafood.

One of the highlights of our food tour in Vientiane, the Laotian capital, is a picnic in Buddha Park by the Mekong River, where we enjoy a mixture of French charcuterie and traditional Laotian snacks. Our interpreter, Ning, always brings these homemade spring rolls with a spicy dipping sauce to the picnic.

75g (2½ oz) dried rice vermicelli
a few drops of sesame oil
16 x 22cm (6 x 8½ in) rice papers
250g (8 oz) cooked pork fillet, cut into thin strips
1 head of soft lettuce, such as mignonette or oak leaf
1 Lebanese cucumber, cut into matchsticks
1 small carrot, cut into matchsticks
½ cup mint leaves
½ cup coriander (cilantro) leaves

Spicy Coconut Vinegar Dipping Sauce
2–8 small red chillies
4 cloves garlic, peeled
1 teaspoon salt
¼ cup (60g/2 oz) white sugar
¼ cup (60ml/2 fl oz) coconut vinegar
¼ cup (60ml/2 fl oz) water
1–2 tablespoons fish sauce
squeeze of fresh lime juice
2 tablespoons roasted and finely crushed peanuts

Place noodles in a bowl and cover with hot water until softened. Strain and rinse in cold water. When well-drained, toss with a few drops of sesame oil and set aside.

Fill a large bowl with hot water and soak the rice papers until just soft. Place a soft rice paper on the bench and then add a piece of lettuce, some of the noodles, a few pieces of carrot and cucumber, a strip of pork and a few mint and coriander leaves. Fold the sides of the roll over the filling and then roll from bottom to top to form a tight roll. Repeat.

Note: After soaking rice papers, if possible hang them off the edges of the kitchen bench. Leave for about 10 minutes and then come back and start rolling. Drying them out slightly makes the process easier.

To make dipping sauce: In a mortar and pestle, pound the chillies, garlic and salt to a paste. Transfer to a bowl and add the sugar, vinegar, water and fish sauce. The sauce should be hot, sour, sweet and salty. Adjust to taste with the sugar and fish sauce. Just before serving, squeeze in the lime juice and add the peanuts.

Seafood Satay with Peanut and Lime Dipping Sauce

Makes 12 satays

The word 'satay' is from a Chinese term meaning 'three pieces', but after watching some of the men in my cooking classes make satays, it seems to mean shove-as-much-meat-on-a-stick-as-possible. Jokes aside, when you buy satay at the markets in South-East Asia, there are just a few bits of skewered meat which always have a delicious smoky flavour from being grilled (broiled) over charcoal. The usual condiments are the ever-popular peanut sauce, a few chunks of cucumber and red onion, while my favourite Singapore satay comes with cubes of pressed rice.
The following deluxe version is made with king prawns (shrimp) and fish and served with a peanut and lime dipping sauce.

12 bamboo skewers, soaked overnight in water
300g (10 oz) meaty fish, like mahi mahi, cut into strips
6 large king prawns (shrimp), peeled, de-veined and tails left on
2 teaspoons roasted coriander (cilantro) seeds
1 teaspoon roasted cumin seeds
¼ teaspoon whole white pepper
½ teaspoon ground turmeric
1 tablespoon ginger, peeled and chopped

2 cloves garlic, peeled
2 stalks lemongrass, bottom half only with outer leaves removed, then sliced finely
2 coriander (cilantro) roots, washed and chopped
pinch of salt
2 teaspoons light palm sugar
1 tablespoon fish sauce
½ cup (125ml/4 fl oz) coconut milk

Divide the fish between 12 skewers, then skewer the prawns pushing the satay stick down the centre of the prawn. Place in a single layer in a glass or ceramic baking dish. Pour the marinade over, making sure the seafood is well-coated. Refrigerate for up to 2 hours.

To make marinade: Grind the coriander seeds, cumin and pepper in a mortar. Add the turmeric, ginger, garlic, lemongrass, coriander roots and salt. Pound to a paste. Transfer to a bowl with the palm sugar, fish sauce and coconut milk, stirring well to dissolve the palm sugar.

To cook: Chargrill the satays on a hot barbecue (grill) for a few minutes on each side. Transfer to a serving plate and serve with the Peanut and Lime Dipping Sauce (see page 48).

Salads

Thai salads are infinite in their variety, running from simple and rustic to the height of fine dining where great importance is placed on knife skills and balance of flavours. Often on Thai menus the list of salads will be more extensive than the other dishes, with many variations on a theme. Thai salads are designed to tantalise the palate and, of all the Thai dishes, the salads are some of my favourites.

The key to making a great Thai salad is to use fresh lime juice. If limes are out of season and too expensive, use lemon juice. (Even though lemon is not really a good substitute, it is far preferable to bottled lime juice with its bitter-tasting preservatives.) Garlic and chillies are often combined in a paste—again, fresh is the key—to which the lime juice is added.

Fresh herbs are one of the common threads in Thai salads and under no circumstance substitute herbs from a tube, or dried herbs. If you can't get fresh Thai basil, use sweet basil, or a variety of any mint, just as long as it's fresh.

Broadly speaking, Thai salads come in three styles—Yam, which means to mix together, Larb which is made from minced (ground) or chopped ingredients, and Som Tam, which is a pounded sour salad.

All Thai salads are very lively and versatile, sometimes eaten as a snack with drinks, but often served as part of a selection of dishes and eaten with rice. The main ingredient is always freshly cooked and the dish served warm or at room temperature. Some very simple rustic salads, like Larb, are served with a large platter of various herbs, wedges of cabbage, cucumber, snake beans and apple eggplant (aubergine).

Once you have an understanding of Thai salad techniques, take the foundations of the recipe, which are the dressing and the herbs, then give it your own touch.

Seafood Salad from Krabi

Serves 6–8 as part of a selection of dishes

I had this simple salad at a rustic cafe in Southern Thailand a few years ago. It has always stayed in my mind because of the attention to detail. The squid and prawns (shrimp) had been bought at the market that morning. The seafood was quickly blanched and tossed with a handful of herbs and chillies. But what I really remember is that I could still smell the perfume in the lime juice, as it had been freshly squeezed minutes before coming out to my table. Easy to recreate at home—just open a cold Singha beer and you could be on holiday in Krabi.

This simple salad can be made more complex with the addition of finely chopped lemongrass, shredded kaffir lime leaves or chopped Chinese celery, and the dressing could be given more depth with the addition of a few cleaned and scraped coriander (cilantro) roots.

250g (8 oz) green prawn meat
250g (8 oz) squid, cleaned and scored
4 small green birdseye chillies (use larger de-seeded (pitted) chillies if mild is preferred)
2 cloves garlic, peeled
¼ cup (60ml/2 fl oz) lime juice
2–3 tablespoons fish sauce
pinch of white sugar
¼ cup mint leaves
¼ cup coriander (cilantro) leaves
2 tablespoons golden shallots, thinly sliced (if unavailable use red onion)
1 medium red chilli, thinly sliced
lettuce for serving

Bring a large pot of water to the boil, add a few teaspoons of salt and quickly blanch the prawns. They will only take about 30 seconds. Bring the water back to the boil and add the squid, removing when it has curled and become opaque. This will only take about 15 seconds. Place seafood in a bowl and toss with the dressing, herbs, shallots and red chilli. Line the serving plate with lettuce and transfer salad to the plate.

To make the dressing: Make a rough paste in a mortar and pestle with the green chillies and garlic, add the lime juice and fish sauce. Season with a pinch or two of sugar. The dressing should be hot, sour and salty.

Coconut Poached Chicken, Prawn and Wing Bean Salad

Serves 6–8 as part of a selection of dishes

I enjoyed this salad in Pak Chong, a major agricultural area an hour or so from Bangkok. It was described on the menu as Wing Bean Salad and the waitress recommended it as being a speciality of the area. What the menu didn't tell us was that it also contained poached chicken, prawns (shrimp), quail eggs and a delicious mild creamy dressing using roasted chilli paste. Very fine knife work was used to shred young ginger and kaffir lime leaves, and the dish was finished with the addition of freshly cooked, crispy shallots. You can make this complex or keep it simple—you decide. The delicious dressing is the key to this dish. Some cooked shredded chicken meat or cooked prawns tossed with the dressing and a handful of fresh herbs would still make a fabulously vibrant Thai salad.

150g (5 oz) peeled green prawn (shrimp) meat
250g (8 oz) chicken breast, sliced into about 4 pieces
1 cup (250ml/8 fl oz) coconut milk
1 cup (250ml/8 fl oz) chicken stock (see page 124) or water
1 tablespoon palm sugar
1 tablespoon fish sauce

2 golden shallots, peeled and sliced
1 quantity of salad dressing
2 tablespoons coconut cream
½ large red chilli, de-seeded (pitted) and julienned finely
2 tablespoons Crispy Golden Shallots (see page 29)
2 tablespoons peanuts

Salad
Cooked prawns (shrimp) and finely shredded chicken
6–8 boiled and peeled quail eggs, or 3–4 hard-boiled chicken eggs, peeled and quartered
1 cup (250g/8 oz) wing beans, cut into 1 cm (½ in) pieces and lightly blanched (if unavailable use green beans, snake beans or asparagus)
2 tablespoons ginger, peeled and shredded very finely
6 kaffir lime leaves, cut into very fine slivers, discarding the central stem

Dressing
1 tablespoon light palm sugar
1 tablespoon water
75ml (2½ fl oz/¹/3 cup) coconut cream
1 teaspoon roasted chilli paste
1 tablespoon fish sauce
2 tablespoons lime juice

To poach prawns and chicken: Combine coconut milk, stock, palm sugar and fish sauce in a saucepan. Bring to a simmer and then add the prawns (shrimp) over a low heat for a few minutes until cooked. Remove with a slotted spoon and set aside.

Add the chicken breast meat and press a piece of baking paper on the surface (don't cover with a lid), then simmer on very low for about 10 minutes. Turn off heat and let chicken cool completely in the coconut milk. When cool, remove from saucepan and shred finely.

To assemble salad: In a bowl, combine the prawns, chicken, eggs, wing beans, ginger, kaffir lime leaves, golden shallots and salad dressing. Toss gently to combine, transfer to serving plate, spoon over the coconut cream and garnish with the red chilli, peanuts and Crispy Golden Shallots.

To make dressing: In a pan, dissolve the palm sugar and water, add the coconut cream, roasted chilli paste and fish sauce. Cook on a low heat until combined. Remove from the heat, cool slightly and then stir in the lime juice.

Spicy Citrus Marinated Scallops with Young Ginger, Coconut and Mint

Serves 6–8 as part of a selection of dishes

Leigh Darlington, one of the restaurant's many talented chefs, put this amazing salad on the menu a few summers ago. It uses the technique of cooking the scallops first with the citrus juice, then tossing with the other ingredients. Impressive first course for a Thai-style meal or as part of a banquet.

Scallop Marinade
24 medium scallops, cut in half horizontally
2 large red chillies, chopped
2 cloves garlic, peeled
pinch of salt
350ml (12 fl oz/1½ cups) lime juice
150ml (5 fl oz/³/₅ cup) orange juice

Scallop Dressing
2–3 small red chillies, chopped
1 clove garlic
75ml (2½ fl oz/¹/₃ cup) fish sauce
75g (2½ oz/¼ cup) light palm sugar
125ml (4 fl oz/½ cup) lime juice
125ml (4 fl oz/½ cup) orange juice

Scallop Salad
marinated scallops
¼ cup shredded fresh coconut
1 large red chilli, de-seeded (pitted) and julienned
½ cup mint leaves
½ cup basil leaves
½ cup coriander (cilantro) leaves
¼ cup ginger, finely shredded
6 kaffir lime leaves, finely shredded
1 quantity of dressing
lettuce leaves for serving

To make marinade: Pound garlic and chillies with the salt. Transfer to a bowl and stir in the lime and orange juice.

Marinate scallops for 20 minutes only and then drain.

To make dressing: Make a paste with the chillies and garlic and transfer to a bowl with the palm sugar, fish sauce, lime juice and orange juice.

To assemble salad: Combine scallops, coconut, chilli, mint, basil, coriander leaves, ginger, lime leaves, lettuce and dressing in a large bowl. Toss gently to combine and transfer to serving platter or individual plates if preferred.

Tangy Salad of Smoked Chicken, White Radish, Mint and Tamarind

Serves 6–8 as part of a selection of dishes

This recipe is inspired by Makphet Restaurant, where I enjoyed a similar version which used smoked fish. The restaurant is in Vientiane, the capital of Laos, and lunch at Makphet is always a highlight of our Laotian tour. The restaurant trains street kids in all aspects of hospitality, giving them a chance at a career in the developing tourism industry.
This dish can be varied at whim. Cucumber or green papaya can replace the white radish, and using grilled (broiled) or barbecued (grilled) chicken can simplify the dish. An oily fish like mackerel, or even salmon, would work beautifully instead of the smoked chicken. The strength of the tea flavour will be determined by the smoking time. The tea can also be replaced with smoking chips bought from barbecue (grill) shops, but the flavour will not be as strong.

500g (1 lb) skinless chicken breast
½ cup (125g/4 oz) brown sugar
½ cup jasmine rice
¼ cup black tea

Dressing

2 tablespoons light palm sugar
2 tablespoons fish sauce
3 tablespoons thick tamarind water (made from 2 tablespoons tamarind mixed with ½ cup (125ml/4 fl oz) boiling water)
1 tablespoon lime juice, use kaffir lime juice if available

Salad

1 quantity of smoked chicken
2 cups shredded or grated white radish
6 hard-boiled and peeled quail eggs, optional
½ cup mint leaves
½ cup Thai basil leaves
1 large red chilli, de-seeded (pitted) and shredded
2 golden shallots

To smoke the chicken: Line a baking tray with several layers of foil, turning up the sides. Mix the tea, sugar and rice together and sprinkle over the base of the baking dish. Place wire cake rack in the tray and place over a preheated barbecue (grill) until the sugar starts to smoke. Place the chicken on the baking rack, cover with a lid and smoke over a moderate heat for 5–10 minutes. Finish off in a 180°C (350°F/Gas Mark 4) oven until just cooked. Shred when cool.

To make dressing: In a bowl, combine the palm sugar, fish sauce, tamarind water and lime juice. The dressing should taste tangy, a little salty and sweet. Adjust to suit your palate.

To make salad: In another bowl, combine remaining ingredients and pour the dressing over, toss gently to mix and then transfer to a serving platter.

Chiang Mai Larb of Duck Breast

Serves 8 as part of a selection of dishes

Another rustic salad that has almost infinite variations is Larb, which is a minced (ground) salad, often served in Australia in cups of lettuce like Chinese Sang Choi Bow. Traditionally, larb always comes with a big side plate of herbs and raw seasonal vegetables and, being from the north-east, is eaten with sticky rice. Its distinctive flavour comes from the addition of roasted rice powder, roasted chilli powder and, again, lots of herbs like mint, coriander (cilantro) and Chinese celery.
Larb can be made with minced (ground) fish, tofu, pork, chicken, beef or even vegetables like mushrooms, all of which offer some brilliant variations.
The following version is a modern adaptation, using sliced duck breast.

4 duck breasts
1 tablespoon sweet soy sauce
3 golden shallots, finely sliced
1 tablespoon lemongrass, tender part only, finely sliced
1 tablespoon finely sliced kaffir lime leaf
4 tablespoons lime juice
2 tablespoons fish sauce

1 teaspoon roasted chilli powder
½ cup mint leaves
½ cup coriander (cilantro) leaves
1–2 fresh red chillies, finely chopped
2 tablespoons roasted rice powder
lettuce leaves for serving

Preheat oven to 200°C (400°F/Gas Mark 6). Dry duck breasts with paper towel and coat with the sweet soy sauce. Heat a non-stick pan to medium and fry the duck breast, skin side down, for a few minutes. Turn and cook on the other side for a few minutes. Transfer to a baking tray and cook in preheated oven for about 10 minutes. Remove from oven and when cool cut into thin slices.

Place sliced duck in a large bowl and add the shallots, lemongrass, kaffir lime leaf, lime juice, fish sauce, chilli powder, mint, coriander, chillies and roasted rice powder. Toss to combine and transfer to serving plate lined with lettuce leaves.

Serve the larb with a platter of mixed herbs like mint, basil and coriander and a selection of chopped raw vegetables such as cabbage, cucumber and beans. For real authenticity also serve with sticky rice.

Waterfall Beef

Serves 6–8 as part of a selection of dishes

This is one of the best-known Thai beef salads, along with Crying Tiger Salad. The sizzling sound of the beef grilling (broiling) over charcoal is supposed to sound like the rushing water of a waterfall. Crying Tiger is so named because the heat of the dish can apparently make a tiger cry. Both are equally delicious and simple and like so many salads that have their origins in the north, are usually served with a side plate of vegetables like cabbage, snake beans and cucumber.

Often in the class when we are searing a good quality cut of beef, someone wants to get the tongs, poke it a few times, and turn it too early. The point of sealing meat is to form a crust that holds in the juices, so not searing well enough often results in the meat stewing. A large portion of meat will cook more evenly in the oven than on a stove top. After the meat is removed from the oven, the juices tend to pool in the centre and the muscle fibres are tight. Resting allows the fibres to relax and the juices to spread through the piece of meat.

500g (1 lb) beef rump or eye fillet
4 golden shallots, peeled and sliced
¼ cup mint
¼ cup coriander (cilantro)
¼ cup Chinese celery (optional)
2 tablespoons roasted rice powder
1 teaspoon roasted chilli powder

Dressing
1 tablespoon white sugar
1/3 cup lime juice
1/3 cup fish sauce
2–6 small red chillies, chopped

Lightly oil a heavy-based frypan or barbecue grill plate and heat to very hot. Sear beef on all sides, then transfer to hot oven and cook to taste. For medium–rare, 500g (1 lb) should take about 7–10 minutes, depending on your oven. Remove from oven and rest, covered, for about 10 minutes. Then slice thinly and toss with the dressing and remaining salad ingredients. Transfer to serving plate.

To make dressing: Combine dressing ingredients in a bowl. It should taste hot, sour and salty.

Crispy Rice Fish and Green Mango Salad

Serves 6–8 as part of a selection of dishes

A few years ago in Bangkok, I was invited to dine with Suvit and Voravan, good friends of my employers, Helen and Peter Brierty. Thais are one of the world's consummate foodies, so it came as no surprise when Suvit said he had been thinking all day about what to order, so we could enjoy some unusual and diverse Thai dishes. One of the first dishes was called rice fish, which I thought sounded very intriguing, but when it arrived, I realised it was what we know as whitebait. The fish came as a crispy tangle, fried in a light-as-air rice flour batter and tossed with a tangy green mango salad. Washed down with a cold Singha beer, I remember thinking, 'Could my job get any better than this?'

Crispy Rice Fish
250g (8 oz) whitebait
100g (3½ oz) rice flour
100g (3½ oz) plain flour
250–300ml (8–10 fl oz) soda water
extra rice flour for dusting
4 cups (1 L/34 fl oz) vegetable oil, such as sunflower or peanut, for frying

Dressing
2–4 medium green chillies, chopped
2 tablespoons fish sauce
5 tablespoons lime juice
1 tablespoon light palm sugar

Green Mango Salad
2 green mangoes, peeled and julienned
2 golden shallots, peeled and thinly sliced
¼ cup mint leaves
¼ cup coriander (cilantro) leaves
¼ cup roasted peanuts or cashews, coarsely crushed

To make the fish: Spread the whitebait on paper towel and dry well. To make the batter, combine the rice and plain flour in a bowl, then lightly whisk in the soda water until it's the consistency of pouring cream. Don't be tempted to make it too thick. Toss the whitebait in the extra flour and then tip handfuls in the batter; deep-fry until crispy and pale golden, about 4–5 minutes.

Drain on paper towel and serve by breaking up the fish into large pieces and tossing briefly with Green Mango Salad.

To make dressing: Crush the chillies in a mortar and then transfer to a bowl with the remaining ingredients. Stir to dissolve the sugar.

To assemble salad: In a large bowl, combine the salad ingredients and the dressing. Toss briefly. Transfer to serving plate.

Tangy Eggplant Salad with Pork and Tamarind

Serves 4 or 6–8 as part of a selection of dishes

This recipe is from a Thai salad class created by chef Katrina Ryan, who shares the teaching load with Annette in the cooking school.

1 large eggplant (aubergine)
½ cup coriander (cilantro) leaves
½ cup golden shallots, peeled and sliced
½ cup fried peanuts
1 large red chilli, seeded (pitted) and cut diagonally into strips
2 tablespoons vegetable oil
2 cloves garlic, peeled and chopped
250g (8 oz) pork mince (ground)
3 tablespoons palm sugar
2 tablespoons fish sauce
4 tablespoons thick tamarind water (see page 25)
1 tablespoon lime juice
½ teaspoon roasted chilli powder
½ cup Thai basil leaves
prawn crackers (Indonesian krupuks), to serve
coriander (cilantro) sprigs for garnish

Cut the eggplant into 2cm thick slices and sprinkle with a little salt. Set aside for 30 minutes then pat dry. Coat well with vegetable oil and bake at 180°C (350°F/Gas Mark 4) for approximately 30 minutes until browned and cooked through. You may need to turn the pieces over after 15 minutes. When cooled, cut into 2cm cubed pieces. Place in a large bowl with the coriander leaves, shallots, peanuts and red chilli strips.

When ready to serve, heat the oil in a wok and fry the garlic till sizzling, then add the pork. Fry well until the pork is cooked through. Add the palm sugar, fry for a few minutes, then add the fish sauce and tamarind. Lastly add the lime juice, chilli powder and basil leaves. Stir-fry until the basil is wilted. Gently toss with the eggplant mixture and serve in bowls, garnished with coriander sprigs and prawn crackers.

Barbecued Cuttlefish Salad with Snow Peas and Lemongrass

Serves 6–8 as part of a selection of dishes

This dish is almost a one-bowl wonder, with a diverse mix of crisp and fresh vegetables tossed with delicious chargrilled cuttlefish. It also demonstrates how red curry paste is used in Thai cooking as a seasoning for a vast array of dishes.

500g (1 lb) cleaned cuttlefish or squid
2 teaspoons rice or corn flour
2 teaspoons Shaoxing wine
2 cloves garlic, peeled and crushed
2 teaspoons ginger, grated
3 tablespoons vegetable oil

Dressing
2 teaspoons red curry paste
2 cloves garlic, peeled and crushed
½ cup (125ml/4 fl oz) lime juice
½ cup (125ml/4 fl oz) fish sauce
4 tablespoons light palm sugar
2 tablespoons roasted rice powder

Salad
100g (3½ oz) baby cos lettuce leaves
½ red capsicum (sweet pepper), julienned
½ green capsicum (sweet pepper), julienned
100g (3½ oz) snow peas (mange tout), topped, tailed and julienned
1/3 cup lemongrass, bottom half only and outer leaves removed, finely sliced
½ red onion, sliced
¼ cup mint leaves
¼ cup coriander (cilantro) leaves
2 tomatoes, cut into wedges
1 small Lebanese cucumber, sliced

To marinate cuttlefish: Mix together the rice or corn flour, wine, garlic, ginger and oil, add cuttlefish and marinate for 2 hours.

To make dressing: Mix ingredients in a bowl until the sugar is dissolved.

To make salad: Heat the barbecue (grill) to hot and grill (broil) cuttlefish until just cooked. This should take about 5 minutes. Combine in a bowl with the dressing and salad ingredients. Transfer to serving plate.

Chinese New Year Salad

Serves 6-8 as part of a selection of dishes

I have taught many variations on Chinese New Year Salad in my classes over the years. Though traditionally served at New Year, it's delicious at any time and with any Asian meal.

Use your imagination as the salad is more about technique than precise ingredients—I have used many varieties of vegetables when serving this as a side dish. Beans, fresh baby corn, celery and capsicum (sweet pepper) all work well. Fresh shredded Chinese cabbage can be tossed through in the final stages along with other herbs like mint, basil or Vietnamese mint. If you like some bite, add fresh red or green chillies.

½ cup (125ml/4 fl oz) rice or coconut vinegar
½ cup (125ml/4 fl oz) water
1 cup (250g/8 oz) white sugar
1 teaspoon salt
1 cup carrot, shredded
1 cup white radish, shredded
1 cup cucumber, shredded
1 small red onion, thinly sliced
2 tablespoons ginger, finely shredded
1 cup bean sprouts, topped and tailed
8 kaffir lime leaves, centre rib removed and finely shredded

½ cup coriander (cilantro) leaves
½ cup mint leaves
1 tablespoon toasted sesame seeds

Dressing
2 tablespoon Chinese plum sauce
2 teaspoon white sugar
pinch of salt
2 tablespoons warm water
2 tablespoons lime juice
1 teaspoon sesame oil

To make salad: Combine the vinegar, water, sugar and teaspoon of salt in a saucepan and bring to the boil, stirring occasionally. When the sugar has dissolved, remove from heat and cool.

In a bowl, mix together the carrot, radish, cucumber, onion and ginger. Pour over the cooled vinegar syrup and allow to pickle for at least 2 hours. This can be done the day before and refrigerated until needed.

Drain the pickled vegetables from the liquid and transfer to a bowl along with the bean sprouts, kaffir lime leaves, coriander and mint leaves. Pour over the dressing and mix to combine, transfer to a serving plate and sprinkle with the sesame seeds.

To make dressing: Combine all ingredients in a bowl and whisk together.

Roast Duck, Pomelo and Mint Salad

Serves 6–8 as part of a selection of dishes

Roast duck can be bought in Chinatown. Some supermarkets also sell pre-cooked Chinese-style duck pieces. If duck is unavailable, use pork fillets and marinate in sweet soy sauce (kecap manis) with a pinch of five-spice powder, then simply grill (broil) or barbecue (grill).
Pomelo is the largest fruit from the citrus family and is available during the winter months. It's similar in flavour to grapefruit, which is a perfect substitute, or use other seasonal fruit. During summer, lychees would be fabulous or even a sweet pineapple would make a brilliant contrast with the rich duck meat.

350g (12½ oz) roast duck meat, sliced
½ pomelo (or 1 grapefruit) peeled, skin and pith removed and shredded into large chunks
2 spring onions (scallions), thinly sliced
2 tablespoons peeled ginger, julienned
½ cup mint leaves
½ red large red chilli, de-seeded (pitted) and julienned
2 teaspoons sesame seeds, roasted

Dressing
2 tablespoons plum sauce
1 tablespoon palm sugar
2 tablespoons Chinese black vinegar
4 tablespoons light soy sauce
½ teaspoon sesame oil

Toss the duck, pomelo, spring onions, ginger, mint, chilli and dressing in a bowl. Transfer to a serving platter and sprinkle with the sesame seeds.

To make dressing: Combine the dressing ingredients in a bowl and mix to dissolve the sugar.

Glass Noodle Salad with Chicken and Prawns

Serves 6–8 as part of a selection of dishes

Glass noodles are made from mung bean starch, and are often labelled 'vermicelli'. They turn transparent when soaked and have little taste, but are used for their bouncy texture and ability to soak up other flavours. Vermicelli noodles can also be made from rice flour, but these have a different texture and tend to go mushy if overcooked. To make sure you have the correct noodles for this dish, just read the list of ingredients on the packet and look for green beans or mung beans, not rice.

125g (4 oz) glass noodles, soaked in boiling water until soft and translucent (about 10 minutes), then drained
6–8 large cooked prawns (shrimp), peeled and de-veined and cut into bite-sized pieces
250g (8 oz) cooked chicken meat, cut into bite-sized pieces
2 stalks lemongrass, bottom half only and outer leaves discarded, very thinly sliced
2 spring onions (scallions), thinly sliced including some of the green top
2–4 small red chillies, or 1 large, finely chopped (de-seed if mild preferred)
½ cup mint leaves
½ cup coriander (cilantro) leaves
½ baby cos lettuce, finely shredded
1 tablespoon Crispy Golden Shallots

Dressing
6 tablespoons lime juice
2 tablespoons fish sauce
1 tablespoon roasted chilli paste
1 tablespoon light palm sugar

To assemble salad: In a large bowl, toss the noodles, prawns, chicken, lemongrass, spring onions, chillies, mint and coriander. Add the dressing and toss to combine.

Line serving plate or bowl with the shredded lettuce and mound the noodle salad on top.

Garnish with the Crispy Golden Shallots (see page 29).

To make dressing: Combine all dressing ingredients in a bowl and stir to dissolve sugar.

Stir-Fries

Over years of doing classes, whenever the word stir-fry is mentioned, all ears seem to prick up. It really should be one of the easiest of all the Thai dishes to recreate at home, requiring no great technical skills or expertise at balancing flavours. But it's also one technique that doesn't translate well to our Western style of eating, where each person is accustomed to being served a big plate of food.

Thailand is a rice-based food culture, where a plate of rice is the focus of the meal, and a selection of dishes, often highly seasoned, are eaten in small quantities with the rice. So a Thai housewife making dinner for her family will only cook one serve of stir-fry which will be shared, along with other dishes like the curry, soup and salad—and all will be eaten with rice.

The key to success is heat. A gas burner is vital, the larger the better. A cheap, thin metal wok will do a much better job than an expensive stainless steel one.

Beef is not a common meat for stir-frying in Thailand, unlike pork and chicken. But it's certainly a cut of meat most Australians love. Judging from class feedback, stir-frying beef for our meat-loving families creates problems due to the large portions we try to cook. More expensive cuts like rump, sirloin and especially eye fillet, need to be seared in a hot wok and cooked very quickly. Fat in meat keeps it moist and carries flavours. So when we stir-fry 500g (1 lb) of lean meat, which on average feeds about four people, the wok loses its heat when the meat goes in, so instead of sealing and holding in the juices, the meat stews and becomes dry very quickly.

If you use a richer cut, that is one with more fat, it will be far more forgiving, stay moist and carry more flavour. So it's a choice between the healthy option or the optimum flavour. If stir-frying for a crowd, chicken thigh meat will give you a brilliant result as the sauce can be reduced without overcooking the meat. If stir-frying for one or two people, there should be no problem using the leaner cuts like chicken breast or pork fillet, as the wok won't be overloaded and lose its heat.

A judicious amount of oil is also necessary for heat to seal the meat or vegetables. Use about 1 tablespoon of oil for every serve. A major principle of stir-fry is 'keep it simple'. It's not necessary to use every sauce in the pantry with an Asian label— sweet chilli sauce won't automatically make your dish Thai! A combination of two sauces, like fish or oyster sauce balanced with some palm sugar, is all it takes to season a delicious stir-fry. Other flavours are added by using herbs, chillies and aromatics like garlic and ginger.

Keep in mind that not all vegetables are suitable for stir-frying. The best varieties are those that need only a short cooking time and don't have a high water content. Add vegetables like sugar snap peas, asparagus, baby corn, julienned carrot or capsicum (sweet pepper) and green beans. All these vegetables just need to be thrown in at the last minute for colour and crunch.—A.F.

Crispy Fish Stir-Fried with Curry Paste, Wild Ginger and Green Peppercorns

Serves 6–8 as part of a selection of dishes

To simplify this dish, the deep-fried fish pieces can be substituted with stir-fried strips of chicken, pork or beef. Prawns (shrimp) and squid also make a great alternative.

Krachai is a variety of ginger referred to in English as 'wild ginger'. It has a distinctive earthy flavour with a musk-like perfume. Both krachai and green peppercorns are difficult to source fresh, but the imported pickled versions from Thailand make a great substitute. They can be left out, but if you want to expand your knowledge of Thai cuisine, they're worth using as both are very common ingredients in stir-fries and curries.

350g (12½ oz) good quality fresh fish, cut on the diagonal into thin medallions
corn or rice flour for dusting
2 cups (500ml/17 fl oz) vegetable oil for deep-frying
2 extra tablespoons vegetable oil
2 tablespoons red curry paste (see page 13)
1–2 tablespoons light palm sugar
1–2 tablespoons fish sauce
1–2 tablespoons water
1 tablespoon shredded krachai, fresh or pickled, rinsed of brine
1 tablespoon pickled green peppercorns, rinsed of brine
10 kaffir lime leaves
½ cup basil leaves

Toss the fish pieces in the rice or corn flour. Heat the oil in a wok to a medium heat. Deep-fry the fish in batches until crispy and golden. If the fish has been cut thinly, this should only take 3–4 minutes. Drain on paper towel and repeat until all the fish is cooked.

Drain oil from wok and set aside. Wipe out the wok, add the extra oil and heat to moderate before adding the red curry paste. Fry gently until fragrant, then add the palm sugar, fish sauce and water. Bring to the boil and simmer until palm sugar has dissolved. Add the krachai, green peppercorns and kaffir lime leaves. Simmer a few minutes and then toss through all the fish.

Lastly, add the basil and as soon as the leaves wilt, remove from the heat.

Stir-Fried Pork with Green Peppercorns and Holy Basil

Serves 8 as part of a selection of dishes

A rustic, fiery stir-fry which is available in food markets all over Thailand. It is usually served with rice and often topped off with a fried egg. If holy basil is unavailable, use Thai basil or mint. Beef and chicken can also be used for this dish if preferred.

8 cloves garlic, peeled and chopped
2 medium chillies, red or green, sliced
2–6 small birdseye chillies, red or green, sliced
2 tablespoons vegetable oil
2 golden shallots, peeled and sliced
500g (1 lb) pork mince (ground)
1 tablespoons fish sauce
1 tablespoon soy sauce
1 tablespoon palm sugar
1 tablespoon sweet soy sauce
1 tablespoon fresh green peppercorns, or use tinned if fresh are unavailable
1 cup holy basil leaves
lime wedges

Make a paste with the garlic and chillies. Heat oil in a wok to medium and cook the paste for a minute. Add the shallots and cook until they start to soften. Add the pork mince and stir-fry for a few minutes. Next add the fish sauce, soy sauce, palm sugar, sweet soy sauce and green peppercorns. Keep cooking until the sauces have combined and the meat is cooked.

Stir the basil through and remove from heat. Transfer to plates and serve with lime wedges.

Crispy Garlic and Pepper Chicken with Snow Peas and Oyster Sauce

Serves 4 or 6—8 as part of a selection of dishes

The combination of garlic, pepper and coriander (cilantro) root is essentially Thai and is used in simple dishes like fried rice, or as part of more complex recipes like red or green curry paste. Along with chillies, shrimp paste, fish sauce and lime juice, these are the fundamental building blocks for Thai cooking.

Just about any Thai restaurant will have a dish that is finished with crispy garlic and pepper. The recipe can be adapted for any meat or seafood and is usually served with a hot-and-sour style sauce to cut through the richness of the deep-fried garlic. Use fresh garlic and if your garlic is starting to shoot, take a few extra minutes to remove the shoot with a paring knife, otherwise the paste could be bitter.

Crispy Garlic and Pepper Paste

3 coriander (cilantro) roots, washed and scraped
1 teaspoon white peppercorns
2 heads of garlic, peeled
1 teaspoon peeled ginger
pinch of salt

Chicken Stir-Fry

1 cup (250ml/8 fl oz) vegetable oil
500g (1 lb) chicken breast or thigh, cut into stir-frying strips
125g snow peas (mange tout), trimmed
2 tablespoons oyster sauce
1 tablespoon fish sauce
1 teaspoon light palm sugar
handful of coriander (cilantro) leaves to garnish

Chilli and Vinegar Sauce

2 large red chillies, de-seeded (pitted) and chopped

1–2 small red chillies, chopped (optional)

2 cloves garlic, peeled

1 coriander (cilantro) root

1 teaspoon salt

4 tablespoons coconut vinegar

2 tablespoons white sugar

To make paste: In a mortar, pound the coriander, peppercorns, garlic, ginger and salt to a course paste. Set aside.

To cook: Heat the vegetable oil to moderate in a large wok and cook the Crispy Garlic and Pepper Paste until pale golden and crispy. Do not overcook or it will become bitter. Drain on paper towel and set aside.

Drain all but 2 tablespoons of oil and heat wok to high. Then add chicken, stir-frying on high heat until just cooked. Add the snow peas, oyster sauce, fish sauce and palm sugar, cooking until just combined.

Transfer to a serving platter and garnish with crispy garlic and pepper mix and coriander leaves. Serve with Chilli and Vinegar Sauce on the side.

To make sauce: Pound the chillies, garlic, coriander and salt to a paste. Transfer to a bowl, stir in the vinegar and sugar.

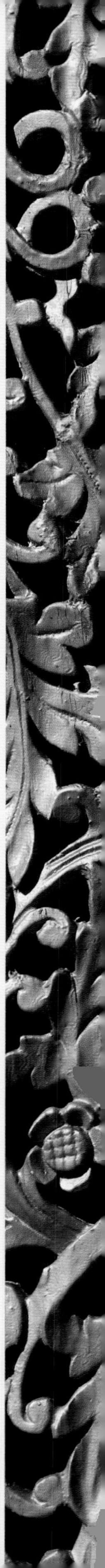

Stir-Fried Asparagus, Sugar Snap Peas and Exotic Mushrooms

Serves 4–6 as a side dish

Even though we tend to think of asparagus as being European, it's a popular vegetable in Thailand and can be found in markets everywhere.

A bewildering range of mushrooms can also be found at produce markets in Thailand, but if all you have available are button mushrooms, then just use them. I like a mix of Swiss browns or shiitake for their intense meaty flavour, oyster mushrooms for their creamy texture and a handful of cloud ears for their unusual, cartilage-like texture.

2 tablespoons vegetable oil
1 bunch asparagus, trimmed, lower stalks peeled with a vegetable peeler and cut into 5cm (2 in) pieces
250g (8oz) mushrooms, sliced
125g (4oz) sugar snap or snow peas (mange tout), topped and tailed
1 tablespoon yellow bean sauce
1 tablespoon oyster sauce
pinch of white sugar
1 teaspoon sesame oil
1 teaspoon sesame seeds

Heat the oil in a wok to almost smoking and add the asparagus and mushrooms. Stir-fry for a few minutes and then add the snow peas, yellow bean sauce, oyster sauce and sugar. Stir-fry another minute and then sprinkle over the sesame oil, stirring to combine. Transfer to a serving plate and sprinkle with sesame seeds.

Stir-Fried Mussels with Chilli Jam, Lemongrass and Pineapple

Serves 6–8 as part of a selection of dishes

You may be thinking that the combination of seafood and fruit is so 1970s, but it's really just very Thai and works brilliantly. The smoky richness of the mussels is offset beautifully by the tart sweet acidity of the pineapple. Just about any seafood can be used this way. Try it and you'll be convinced.

2 tablespoons water
2 stalks lemongrass, outer leaves removed and cut into 5cm (2 in) pieces
10 kaffir lime leaves
2 teaspoons light palm sugar
2 tablespoons fish sauce
3 tablespoons roasted chilli paste
2 large red chillies, de-seeded (pitted) and thinly sliced
1 kg (2.2 lb) black mussels
½ small pineapple, peeled and sliced
½ cup Thai basil leaves
squeeze of fresh lime juice

In a wok put the water, lemongrass, kaffir lime leaves, palm sugar, fish sauce, chilli paste and chillies. Bring to the boil and add the mussels and pineapple, cover and cook until the mussels open. You may need to toss the mussels and pineapple around a few times while cooking. Finish with the basil leaves and a squeeze of lime juice. Transfer to a serving bowl.

Stir-Fried Chinese Cabbage, Water Chestnuts and Black Vinegar

Serves 6–8 as a side dish

This is a brilliantly simple vegetable dish to serve as part of a banquet, or to serve as an everyday vegetable dish together with a meat dish. The black vinegar gives the cabbage a subtle sweet-and-sour note.

2 tablespoons vegetable oil
1 medium carrot, julienned
1 medium brown onion, peeled and thinly sliced
½ Chinese cabbage, shredded
¾ cup water chestnuts, sliced
2 tablespoons black vinegar
1 tablespoon Shaoxing wine
1 teaspoon white sugar
2 tablespoons oyster sauce
1 teaspoon sesame oil

Heat vegetable oil to almost smoking. Add the carrot and onion, stir-fry for a minute and then add the cabbage. Keep stir-frying until the cabbage starts to wilt, about 1–2 minutes.

Now add the water chestnuts, black vinegar, Shaoxing wine, sugar and oyster sauce.

Lastly, mix the sesame oil through then transfer to a serving plate.

Asparagus Tossed with Prawns, Roasted Chilli Paste, Coconut Cream and Crispy Shallots

Serves 4

This is another simple stir-fry highlighting the versatility of roasted chilli paste. Like all recipes, you can make it your own and use chicken or pork instead of prawns (shrimp). Substitute asparagus for any other quick-cooking green vegetable. The key ingredient in this dish is roasted chilli paste.

¼ cup (60ml/2 fl oz) vegetable oil
¼ cup golden shallots, peeled and thinly sliced
2 cloves garlic, peeled and crushed
1 large red chilli, de-seeded (pitted) and sliced
250g (8 oz) green prawn (shrimp) meat
1 bunch of asparagus, trimmed and ends peeled, then sliced on the diagonal into 5cm (2 in) pieces
1 tablespoon roasted chilli paste
2 tablespoons coconut cream
2 tablespoons fish sauce
2 tablespoons lime or lemon juice
2 tablespoons water
1 tablespoon light palm sugar
2 tablespoons roasted and crushed peanuts

In a wok, heat the oil and fry the shallots until golden. Remove with a slotted spoon, drain on paper towel and set aside.

Reheat the oil in the wok and fry the garlic and chilli for a minute or so. Now add the prawns and stir-fry until they are just starting to colour. Add the asparagus and stir-fry briefly. Mix in the roasted chilli paste, coconut cream, fish sauce, lime juice, water and sugar. Cook until combined, then stir in the peanuts.

Transfer to a serving platter and garnish with crispy shallots.

Stir-Fried Chicken with Chilli Paste and Cashews

Serves 6–8 as part of a selection of dishes

I'm prepared to bet that this would be one of the most frequently ordered stir-fry dishes at your suburban Thai take-away ... along with Ginger Chicken. On our Bangkok food tours, this is a frequently requested dish. And what's not to like? It's an easy, everyday dish with the crunchy cashews combining with sweet smoky notes from the chilli paste.

2 tablespoons vegetable oil
4–6 medium dried chillies, optional
6 cloves garlic, peeled and pounded to a coarse paste
2 golden shallots, or half a small onion, peeled and sliced
400g (14 oz) chicken breast or thigh, cut into stir-frying strips
1 tablespoon roasted chilli paste
1 tablespoon oyster sauce
1 tablespoon fish sauce
1 tablespoon light palm sugar
½ cup roasted unsalted cashews
4 spring onions, including some of the green tops, cut into 5cm (2 in) pieces
coriander (cilantro) sprigs to garnish

Place the oil in a wok and heat to medium. Add the chillies and fry briefly until they start to darken. Remove and drain on paper towel. Set aside.

Add the garlic to the oil and cook until just starting to colour. Raise the heat to high and add the golden shallots and chicken strips, stirring constantly for about 2 minutes. Now add the chilli paste, oyster sauce, fish sauce and palm sugar. (You may need to add a tablespoon or so of water if the sauce reduces too quickly.)

Stir-fry for a few more minutes until the chicken is cooked and, lastly, stir through the cashews, green spring onions and fried chillies.

Transfer to serving plate and garnish with coriander sprigs.

Stir-Fry of Ginger Chicken with Mushrooms

Serves 6–8 as part of a selection of dishes

This is ideally cooked when ginger is young. In our Yandina region, the first ginger harvest is around February, but the ginger gets hotter as it's harvested later in the year. If new season ginger is unavailable, old shredded ginger can be rinsed in cold water to tone the bite down if desired.

Serve with the hot-and-sour dipping sauce for a classic Thai dish.

In every class, I make a few small bowls of this traditional condiment so the students can spice up the food to suit their palate. Although this sauce does keep, it's best when freshly made, as the lime juice becomes flat and metallic-tasting if left too long in the fridge. In the restaurant kitchen, our chefs make this sauce afresh every few hours.

2 tablespoons vegetable oil
6 cloves garlic, peeled and crushed to a coarse paste in a mortar with a pestle
3 golden shallots, or 1 small onion, peeled and thinly sliced
400g (14 oz) chicken breast or thigh, cut into stir-frying strips
250g (8 oz) sliced button mushrooms
1 tablespoon sweet soy sauce
1 tablespoon fish sauce
1 tablespoon yellow bean sauce

1 tablespoon coconut or rice vinegar
¼ cup ginger, peeled and finely shredded
4 green spring onions, including some of the green top, cut into 5cm (2 in) pieces

Hot and Sour Dipping Sauce
¼ cup (60ml/2 fl oz) lime juice, or lemon if limes are not available
1–2 tablespoons of fish sauce
2–6 small hot red and green chillies, finely sliced

To make stir-fry: Place oil in a wok and heat to moderate, add garlic and cook until pale golden. Turn the heat to high and add the golden shallots and chicken, stir-frying for a few minutes. Now add the mushrooms and cook for another minute. Add the soy sauce, fish sauce, yellow bean sauce, vinegar and ginger, stir-frying until the chicken is cooked, about 3–4 minutes.

Stir in the green spring onions and transfer to a serving plate. Serve with Hot and Sour Dipping Sauce.

To make dipping sauce: Combine all the ingredients in a bowl.

Lemongrass Spiced Pork with Cloud Ear Mushrooms and Bamboo Shoots

Serves 4 or 6–8 as part of a selection of dishes

The poetically named cloud ear mushroom is more prosaically called wood fungus, as it grows on tree trunks. It is sometimes available fresh from good supermarkets but the dried version is just as suitable. Soak in boiling water for 10 minutes or so, then rinse well to remove any dirt. If unavailable, use button mushrooms which will still result in a delicious stir-fry. The bamboo plant in Asia is very important because of its versatility. It's used in scaffolding, for building houses, making furniture and many cooking utensils. As a bonus, the tender new shoots are edible. Canned bamboo shoots lack the more delicate flavour of the fresh variety, but for practical purposes are all most of us have on hand, so just rinse them a few times in fresh water before using.

2 stalks lemongrass, bottom half and outer leaves removed
good pinch of salt
1 tablespoon ginger, peeled and roughly chopped
2 cloves garlic, peeled
1 tablespoon sweet soy sauce
2 tablespoons vegetable oil
1 small brown onion, peeled and sliced
400g (14 oz) pork, sliced into stir-frying strips
1 cup button mushrooms, sliced

¼ cup dried cloud ear mushrooms, soaked, rinsed and sliced
½ cup bamboo shoots, rinsed
1 tablespoon thin soy sauce
2 tablespoons fish sauce
1 tablespoon rice or coconut vinegar
1–2 teaspoons light palm sugar
2 green spring onions, including some of the green top, thinly sliced
handful of coriander (cilantro) leaves for garnish

Pound the lemongrass with a pestle so it splits. If it doesn't, you may need to remove another layer or so. Be ruthless, as you only want the very tender inner core. Now slice the lemongrass as finely as your knife skills allow. Add the lemongrass, salt, ginger and garlic into a mortar and pound to a paste.

Put the pork in a bowl with the sweet soy sauce and paste, then mix well to coat. Refrigerate for 2 hours.

Heat oil in a wok to high; add the onion and cook, stirring constantly for 30 seconds. Add the pork and stir-fry for a few minutes. Add the button and cloud ear mushrooms and bamboo shoots and keep stir-frying for another minute or so. Now add the soy sauce, fish sauce, vinegar and palm sugar. Keep cooking, constantly stir-frying until the sauces have combined and the pork has cooked. Transfer to serving plate and sprinkle with green spring onions and coriander.

Beef Stir-Fried with Oyster Sauce, Broccoli and Pickled Ginger

Serves 4 or 6–8 as part of a selection of dishes

The origins of this classic stir-fry are certainly Chinese but the Thais, with their usual culinary confidence, have tweaked the dish and added the characteristic flavour of fish sauce. It's usually served with a vinegar and chilli condiment to liven things up.

The condiment is so easy to make and is one of the condiments—along with chilli powder, sugar and fish sauce—found on just about every Thai table. It allows the individual diner to adjust the hot, sour, sweet and salty flavours that are keynotes in Thai food.

Do be bold and use small chillies as they have more intense floral notes compared to larger chillies which are more capsicum (sweet pepper)-like in flavour. A great chilli that has a medium punch and brilliant taste is the Serrano, which can often be found in large supermarkets.

The pickled ginger can be bought in most big supermarkets or just use a tablespoon of shredded fresh ginger and add with the garlic.

Like all stir-fries, don't overload the wok with too much meat or too many vegetables. Other vegetables such as broccolini, cauliflower, asparagus or snow peas (mange tout) work just as well as the broccoli.

2 tablespoons vegetable oil
400g (14 oz) sliced beef rump or fillet
1 small brown onion, thinly sliced
2 cloves garlic, peeled and minced (ground)
2 tablespoons oyster sauce
2 tablespoons fish sauce
2 tablespoons light palm sugar
1–2 tablespoons water

2 cups broccoli florets
2 tablespoons pickled ginger, shredded

Chilli Vinegar Condiment (Phrik Dong Nam Som)
½ cup (125ml/4 fl oz) rice or coconut vinegar
1 tablespoon fish sauce
2–10 small, hot red and green chillies

To make stir-fry: Heat the oil in a wok to smoking, add the beef and stir-fry for a minute to seal. Add the onion and garlic. Stir-fry another minute. Add the oyster sauce, fish sauce, palm sugar and water and keep stir-frying for the sauces to combine. Now add the broccoli and stir-fry briefly. Mix through the pickled ginger and transfer to a serving plate. Serve with Chilli Vinegar Condiment.

To make condiment: Slice chillies and add to a small bowl with the vinegar and fish sauce.

Stir-Fried Beef with Chilli Bean Sauce, Ginger and Tomato

Serves 2–4, or 6–8 as part of a selection of dishes

Tomatoes are another vegetable introduced to Thai cuisine by Portuguese traders—like chillies, pineapple and pawpaw (papaya), tomatoes also came from the Americas. Fresh tomatoes are often added to stir-fry vegetable dishes, fried rice or soups, while tomato sauce can be found in many stir-fries, including the very popular Pad Thai noodles. This is a fantastic beef stir-fry as long as you don't exceed more than about 400g (14 oz) of beef. You could sear the meat in batches, but that defeats the whole point of a stir-fry—that it's fast.

2 teaspoons ginger, peeled and roughly chopped
2 cloves garlic, peeled
2–3 tablespoons vegetable oil
1 medium brown onion, sliced
400g (14 oz) rump steak, cut into stir-frying strips
½ medium carrot, peeled and cut into stir-frying strips
3 teaspoons chilli bean sauce (available from Asian supermarkets)
2 teaspoons tomato sauce
2 teaspoons oyster sauce
2 teaspoons light palm sugar
1 teaspoon sesame oil
2 green spring onions, including some of the green tops, peeled and cut into 5cm (2 in) pieces
1 tomato, cut into thin wedges
1 teaspoon sesame seeds

Make a rough paste with the ginger and garlic in a mortar and pestle.

Heat the oil to medium and add the garlic and ginger paste along with the onion. Stir-fry for a minute and then turn up the heat to high and add the beef. Stir-fry for a few minutes to seal well and then add the carrot, cooking just a minute or so. Now add the chilli bean sauce, tomato sauce, oyster sauce and palm sugar. Cook until the sauces have combined, then add the sesame oil, green spring onions and tomato. Stir to combine and remove from heat. Transfer to a serving plate and sprinkle with sesame seeds.

Stir-Fried Eggplant with Silken Tofu and Pork

Serves 4 or 8 as part of a selection of dishes

There are many eggplant (aubergine) varieties. Small, bitter pea eggplants are popular in Thai curries. Apple eggplants, in a range of colours, are eaten both raw and cooked. Long eggplants, similar to Japanese eggplant but green in colour, are grilled (broiled), stir-fried or used in curries. The Japanese style eggplant is the most suitable if the long green variety is unavailable. I have also used large purple eggplant with success. Just cut into long, thin wedges, salt lightly and sit for an hour or so to disgorge some of the bitter liquid, then rinse well, drying on a paper towel before using.

A flippant comment made in a class was that vegetarians deserve tofu. We all laughed at the expense of my many vegetarian friends, but joking aside, it showed our lack of understanding of how tofu is used in Asian cooking. Tofu, or soy bean curd, is a high protein food. It's low in calories and comes in many varieties—firm with a rubbery texture, silken and delicate like a set custard, strongly flavoured and fermented with red rice, sold as sheets used for wrapping and deep-frying—just to name a few. It's generally used for texture and as a flavour carrier, and is often combined with meat in soups, curries or stir-fries. Phad Thai, one of the best-loved Thai noodle dishes, traditionally includes finely diced firm tofu mixed in with the other ingredients. This stir-fry dish uses firm silken tofu, which is not as delicate as some silken tofu which falls apart as soon as its handled. Most big supermarkets stock an extensive range of tofu. Omit the pork to make a vegetarian stir-fry.

4 tablespoons vegetable oil
125g pork mince (ground)
4 Thai or Japanese-style eggplants (aubergines), cut in quarters lengthways
1 tablespoon ginger, peeled and minced (ground)
2 cloves garlic, peeled and minced (ground)
1 brown onion, thinly sliced
1 red capsicum (sweet pepper), cut into stir-frying strips
1 tablespoon yellow bean sauce

1 tablespoon sweet soy sauce
1 tablespoon thin soy sauce
1 tablespoon rice or coconut vinegar
1 tablespoon light palm sugar
1–2 tablespoons water
250g (8 oz) firm silken tofu, cut into 2½cm (1 in) pieces
2 green spring onions, including some of the green tops, cut into 5cm (2 in) pieces

Heat 1 tablespoon of the oil in a wok and add the mince, stirring to break it up. Remove when cooked and set aside. Wipe out the wok with paper towel and add remaining oil. Heat to smoking and add the eggplant, constantly stir-frying for about 3 minutes to seal well. Add the ginger, garlic and onion and stir-fry a few more minutes. Add the capsicum, yellow bean sauce, sweet soy sauce, soy sauce, vinegar, palm sugar and water. Bring to the boil and then reduce to a simmer. Return the pork mince to the wok and keep cooking until the eggplant has softened and the sauce reduced. Lastly, stir through the tofu and green spring onions, taking care not to break up the tofu too much. Transfer to a serving plate.

Rice

In the water there is fish.
In the fields there is rice.
The king takes no advantage of the people.
Who wants to trade, trades.
The faces of the people shine bright with happiness.

Inscription on Sukhothai Temple, 1292

Rice, the sacred grain, is the staple food for over one and half billion people—and still counting. The daily sustenance for Asian peasants is a bowl of rice with a splash of soy or fish sauce. To have a daily meal which does not include a bowl of rice, is to have not eaten at all. Each grain is sacred—the everyday difference between life and death. Evidence of early rice cultivation, dating back 2000 years, has been found at Ban Chiang in the north-east of Thailand.

Rice is a great source of fibre and vitamins, is cholesterol, fat and sodium free, easy to digest and perfect for those with gluten allergy.

Rice is the most important part of any Thai meal. Curries, relishes, soups and salads are all given the generic name gap kao which translates as 'with rice'. The common greeting in Thailand is not 'How are you?' but 'Gin kao ruu yang?' which literally translates as 'Have you eaten rice yet?'

In China, an 'iron rice bowl' is their modern expression for job security, while losing one's job is referred to as 'breaking the rice bowl'. Rice is used in Madagascar to express time; 'half an hour' translates as 'the time it takes to cook rice'.

Rice is a member of the grass family with the unusual capacity to grow in water. Nutrients are replenished by the constant movement of water and flooded fields need never lie fallow. Consequently, cultivating rice in paddy fields produces far more yield than rice grown on dry land. And rice paddies are also home to other food sources—ducks, frogs, fish and insects.

Because of the huge reliance on water to grow their crop, rice farmers are highly dependent on seasonal rains and must learn to control the flow of water through the use of terraces, canals or dykes. Tending paddy fields is hard and incessant work, requiring many hands, so it demands a high degree of social organisation and cooperation for it to work efficiently. In Bali, a sophisticated system of temple ceremonies has evolved to coordinate the distribution of water to each farmer, and a complex calendar regulates planting and harvesting. Festivals and religious ceremonies are held to support the process and encourage the social aspects of such a close-knit agricultural system.

Rice sustains daily life, but it can also consume it. So when you next eat rice, treat it with the reverence it so justly deserves.

Fried Rice with Pork, Basil and Roasted Chilli Paste

Serves 2

Fried rice is traditionally a one-bowl meal. It is rarely shared, and would never replace steamed rice as the basis of a meal. I have eaten fried rice all over South-East Asia and it has nearly always been eaten at markets or cafes and treated as fast food or a quick snack.

The secret to good fried rice is simple. You need a wok, cooked rice that's a day or so old and, as with all stir-fries, don't cook too much at once. Any meat or seafood can be used in this dish. Holy basil is preferred in Thailand, but if it's not readily available, replace with Thai or sweet basil. You could also use a combination of basil and mint.

3 tablespoons vegetable oil
3 cloves garlic, peeled and crushed
1 small brown onion, peeled and thinly sliced
1–2 small red chillies, sliced
200g (7 oz) pork fillet, sliced thinly
1–2 teaspoons roasted chilli paste (see page 12)
2 tablespoons fish sauce

2 tablespoons soy sauce
1 teaspoon white sugar
2 cups cooked jasmine rice
¼ cup basil leaves
1 tomato, cut into thin wedges
½ small cucumber, thinly sliced
lime wedges to garnish

Heat the oil to moderate in a wok and stir-fry the garlic, onion and chillies for a few minutes. Turn up the heat to high and add the pork, stir-frying until the meat begins to colour. Add the roasted chilli paste, fish sauce, soy sauce and sugar. Stir to combine then mix the rice through. Add the basil leaves and keep stir-frying until the leaves have wilted. Transfer to a serving plate and garnish with the tomato, cucumber and lime wedges.

Perfect Rice

Serves 4

The first thing every young Thai girl learns is how to cook rice, because if she can cook rice, she can make a meal. Long-grained jasmine rice is the preferred rice for most Thais, except those from the north and north-east who prefer sticky rice.

2 cups jasmine rice
3 cups (750ml/26 fl oz) cold water

Wash the rice in several changes of water until the water is fairly clear. Drain well and place in a saucepan or rice cooker.

Cover with water up to the first joint on the index finger. (I used to be sceptical about the knuckle technique, but it is a reliable method.) Don't add salt to the water. Jasmine rice has its own delicate perfume which is destroyed by salt.

If using a saucepan, cover with a lid and bring water to the boil. Reduce heat to low and cook rice without stirring for about 15–20 minutes. Lift the lid to check that it is cooked, cook for 1–2 minutes longer if necessary. The rice is done when the grains are soft enough to crush between your thumb and forefinger. Turn off the heat and let the rice stand covered for 8–10 minutes to absorb the steam before serving.

Sometimes the top of the rice can be a little dry at the end of cooking, as it varies in its ability to absorb water depending on the growing conditions. Just sprinkle on some more water and cook a few more minutes.

FAQ: What's the difference between brown and white rice?
Brown rice is de-husked, unpolished rice and, though rich in nutrients, is considered inferior to white polished rice. In Thailand, brown rice is commonly eaten by poor people or servants and is served in prisons and institutions.

FAQ: How do I cook sticky rice?
Sticky rice is traditionally cooked in a conical woven bamboo basket, but you will achieve a great result using a bamboo steamer basket placed over a wok full of boiling water. First soak the sticky rice either overnight or for a few hours. When ready to cook, rinse a few times, drain off water and spread over a steamer basket that has been lined with muslin or a clean tea towel. Place steamer basket over a wok full of briskly boiling water, cover and cook for 25–30 minutes.

Fried Rice with Crab and Egg

Serves 2

Occasionally fried rice is served as a main dish rather than fast food. One memorable lunch in Pak Chong, I watched as plate after plate of fried rice with crab left the kitchen bound for nearly every table. The presentation certainly wasn't market-style, as the fried rice was wrapped in a lacy egg net tied with garlic chives. This simplified version, though not as elaborate in presentation, is just as delicious, and like most Thai-style fried rice is served with fresh lime and chillies to add some bite.

½ cup (125ml/4 fl oz) vegetable oil
2 golden shallots, peeled and thinly sliced
2 cloves garlic, peeled and crushed
2 eggs, lightly beaten
2 cups cooked jasmine rice
freshly ground white pepper
½ teaspoon white sugar
3 tablespoons soy sauce
1 tablespoon fish sauce
4 green spring onions, including some of the green tops, thinly sliced

200g (7 oz) fresh crabmeat, picked over to remove traces of shell
handful of coriander (cilantro) leaves for garnish

Chilli and Lime Sauce
3 tablespoons lime juice
splash of fish or soy sauce
2–6 small red and green chillies, thinly sliced

Heat the oil in a wok to medium heat and fry the golden shallots until golden and crispy. Drain on paper towel and set aside. Remove all but 3 tablespoons of the oil and gently fry the garlic until just starting to colour. Add the egg and stir to scramble. Add the rice, pepper, sugar, soy sauce and fish sauce. Stir-fry to combine and then fold the spring onions and crabmeat through. Transfer to a serving plate and garnish with the crispy shallots and coriander leaves. Serve with Chilli and Lime Sauce on the side.

To make sauce: Combine all ingredients in a small bowl.

Coconut Rice

Serves 6–8

As it is often on the menu at suburban Thai restaurants, I am frequently asked how to cook coconut rice. With a lush creamy flavour, it's used as a foil for very spicy dishes like pawpaw (papaya) salad and sour curries.
The pandanus leaf is available frozen from good Asian supermarkets. Don't try to substitute the leaves of the pandanus trees that grow along Queensland beaches. Though from the same family, the pandanus that is used in Asian cooking is a clumping plant with long, ribbon-like leaves that grows to about 1 metre tall. Most Thai houses have one growing in their backyard.

2½ cups jasmine rice
2½ cups coconut milk
1½ cups (350ml/12 fl oz) water
2 teaspoons white sugar
pinch of salt
2 pandanus leaves (optional)

Wash rice well in several changes of water. Strain and place in a saucepan with the coconut milk, water, sugar, salt and pandanus leaves. Bring to the boil, covered, stirring once or twice, and then reduce heat to very low. Cook covered without stirring for 20 minutes. The coconut cream will have risen to the top. Stir to combine, discard the pandanus leaves and serve.

Curried Rice with Chicken and Fresh Cucumber Pickle

Serves 4 or 8 as part of a selection of dishes

The first time I enjoyed this was in Hat Yai, a lively but slightly seedy town just over the Thai border from Malaysia. Hat Yai is a mecca for Muslim food, including roti and spice-dominated curries. This is a pilaf-style dish, with the chicken and spices braised in the rice. It's sometimes served with a bowl of broth or a simple pickle.

4 cloves garlic, peeled
2 tablespoons ginger, peeled and chopped
1 tablespoon fresh turmeric, peeled and chopped (if unavailable, use a teaspoon of powdered turmeric)
1 teaspoon salt
1 tablespoon curry powder
4 chicken thighs, cut in half
1 cup (250ml/8 fl oz) vegetable oil
4 golden shallots, peeled and thinly sliced
3 cups jasmine rice, rinsed and drained

4 cups (1 L/34 fl oz) chicken stock (see page 124)
½ cinnamon stick

Cucumber Pickle
½ cup (125ml/4 fl oz) coconut or rice vinegar
¼ cup (60g/2 oz) white sugar
1 teaspoon salt
1 small Lebanese cucumber
2 small golden shallots, peeled and sliced
2–4 small red chillies, thinly sliced

Make a paste with the garlic, ginger, turmeric and salt, then mix with the curry powder. Place chicken in a bowl and coat with the spice paste. Set aside for an hour or two in the refrigerator.

Heat a cup of oil in a wok to medium and fry the shallots until golden and crispy. Drain on paper towel. Transfer 4 tablespoons of the oil into a heavy-based saucepan and brown the chicken. Add the rice, stock and cinnamon. Bring to the boil, stirring once or twice, then turn down to a very low heat, cover and cook for 20 minutes. Transfer to a serving plate and garnish with the reserved crispy shallots. Serve with Cucumber Pickle.

To make pickle: Combine the vinegar, sugar and salt in a saucepan. Take off heat as soon as sugar has dissolved. Allow to cool completely.

Cut the cucumber lengthways and then finely dice. Combine in a bowl with the shallots, chillies and cooled vinegar syrup.

Noodles

Noodle vendors are everywhere in Thailand. From the crowded streets of Bangkok to any small village there will be stalls, cafes and mobile carts selling this most popular fast food of Asia. Like all Thai food, the variety and methods of preparation are infinite. Noodles can be stir-fried over high heat for a delicious smoky flavour, gently cooked in a gravy-like sauce, fried until crispy, or simply blanched and served in a simple soup. On a trip to Thailand many years ago with my husband and son, we took a long tail boat tour around the Bangkok klongs (canals). The boat driver hailed a woman in a smaller boat and she proceeded to cook a dish of fresh rice sheets over a charcoal brazier. She folded the rice sheets over a variety of herbs, then chopped them into small pieces. She then drizzled the noodles with sweet soy, all the time balancing in a tiny boat. So simple, so delicious!

The following selection of noodles can be cooked in the safety of your home kitchen, no sea legs required, but like fried rice and stir-fries, these dishes are best cooked for a maximum of two people. As you increase the quantities, their success will diminish. My suggestion for cooking noodles Western-style for the family is to cook the noodles, divide them between the serving bowls, cook the topping, then portion over the noodles—otherwise you risk ending up with a big gluggy mess.

Pad Thai

Serves 1

I love Pad Thai as much as everyone else but a few years ago I declared, in diva-like fashion, that I would never again do Pad Thai in a class as it always turned into a gluey mess when cooked in large quantities. Despite many requests, I have stuck to my guns, but with this book I have relented and will give instructions on cooking Pad Thai for one. The best known of all the Thai noodle dishes, a vendor can whip up a single plate of Pad Thai in a few minutes. The following recipe is traditional market-style, which means it has no meat or seafood. These can be added at your discretion.

60g (2 oz) dried thin rice noodles
1 tablespoon vegetable oil
1 golden shallot, peeled and sliced
1 egg, lightly whisked
1 tablespoon light palm sugar
1 tablespoon tamarind water
2 tablespoons fish sauce
50g (2 oz) firm bean curd, cut into 1cm (½ in) cubes
1 tablespoon dried shrimp, rinsed
2 teaspoons preserved radish (from Asian supermarkets—omit if unavailable)
½ cup bean sprouts
a few garlic chives or green spring onions, cut into 2½ cm (1 in) pieces
2 tablespoons peanuts, roasted and coarsely crushed
a good pinch of roasted chilli powder (see page 24)
lime wedge

Place noodles in a bowl and cover with hot water. Leave for about half an hour, then drain.

Heat vegetable oil in a wok and stir-fry the shallot until it starts to colour, then add the egg and scramble. Add the palm sugar, tamarind water, fish sauce, bean curd, dried shrimp and radish. Stir to combine. Add the noodles and stir-fry until just starting to colour and soften. Add half the bean sprouts, all of the garlic chives and half the peanuts. Stir-fry until combined. Transfer to a serving plate and garnish with the remaining bean sprouts, peanuts and chilli powder. Serve with the lime wedge.

Singapore-Style Seafood Noodles

Serves 1

Another classic noodle dish that has found its way throughout South-East Asia. I love the combination of chewy Hokkien noodles and bouncy rice vermicelli with the rustic and hearty seafood sauce.

2 tablespoons vegetable oil
3 cloves garlic, peeled and crushed
1 small golden shallot, peeled and sliced
50g (1¾ oz) finely chopped pork fillet
50g (1¾ oz) green prawn (shrimp) meat
50g (1¾ oz) squid, cleaned and sliced
1 egg
1 tablespoon soy sauce
1 tablespoon fish sauce
pinch of white sugar
30g (1 oz) rice vermicelli noodles, soaked in hot water until softened, then drained
60g (2 oz) fresh Hokkien noodles
1–2 tablespoons chicken stock (see page 124) or water
pin of white pepper
¼ cup bean sprouts
a few garlic chives or green spring onions, sliced
½ large red chilli, sliced
lime wedge to garnish

Heat oil to moderate and stir-fry the garlic and shallot until just starting to colour. Add the pork and stir-fry a few minutes, then add the prawn and squid and keep stir-frying for another minute or so. Push to the side of the wok and break in the egg. Scramble briefly and then add the soy sauce, fish sauce and sugar. Stir everything together and then add all the noodles. Add the stock or water and keep cooking until the noodles have softened.

Stir in the white pepper, bean sprouts and garlic chives. Transfer to a serving plate and garnish with chilli and lime wedges.

Stir-Fried Rice Noodles with Chicken and Choy Sum

Serves 1

This everyday noodle dish is a good example of keeping it simple. It is always served with condiments of sugar, chilli powder, and fresh chillies in vinegar and fish sauce so the individual diner can adjust the hot, sour, sweet and salty notes. The fresh rice noodles have a delicious chewy texture and will be available at any good Asian supermarket. Substitute meat or seafood for the chicken.

2 tablespoons vegetable oil
2 cloves garlic, peeled and crushed
125g (4 oz) sliced chicken breast or thigh meat
125g (4 oz) fresh wide rice noodles
a few stems choy sum or other greens cut into 2½ cm (1 in) pieces
1 tablespoon sweet soy sauce
1 tablespoon soy sauce
1 teaspoon oyster sauce
pinch of white pepper
water

Heat the oil to moderate and fry the garlic briefly until just starting to colour. Add the chicken and stir-fry until almost cooked. Add the noodles, choy sum, soy sauces and oyster sauce. Stir-fry until the noodles have softened and the choy sum has wilted. Finish with the white pepper, adding a few splashes of water if necessary.

Food for Thought

Next time you open your favourite cookbook, stop and reflect on what it tells you about the people who created the recipes, because a recipe is much more than a list of ingredients and instructions for cooking a dish.

All recipes reflect a culture and, quite often, a period of history in the country of their origin. Recipes literally tell a story—of the people who grew and stored the ingredients, of the climate, of the local raw materials available to manufacture cooking implements, of foreign influences, of goods traded.

The spices in the Thai Massaman curry recipe, for example, reflect a period in history when Thailand first came into contact with Indian and Arab merchants. These Muslim traders introduced the Thais to food spiced with cardamom and cumin, and gradually traditional Thai recipes were adapted until curries like Massaman (its name derived from 'Muslim man') became part of the everyday repertoire.

In the 1600s, the Portuguese began trading with Thailand. The merchants brought with them hot chillies from South America and also introduced wheat flour and eggs for dessert-making. Waves of Chinese fleeing famine brought with them bamboo steamers and iron woks which consequently opened the door to a greater range of cooking methods based around these different utensils.

The food Australians eat today reflects similar foreign influences on tastes, ingredients, techniques and utensils—all brought about not by trade, but by migrants. At some time every day, we are tasting the influences Asian, European, Arabic, Indian, Chinese and African migrants have had on our diet, and even on our kitchen equipment.

If my grandmother were alive today, she would find my kitchen a most alien place—microwave, woks, bamboo steamers, cappuccino machine, tagine, pasta maker, pizza trays, rice cooker—the list goes on and on, right through to the indispensable mortar and pestle. Peeking inside the pantry or refrigerator, she would probably feel like Alice falling through the rabbit hole into a wondrously strange and exotic foodland!

Australians' daily eating habits are in a constant state of metamorphosis. By drawing on the influences of immigrants' traditional foods, combining them with our wide range of climate and soils suitable for growing a variety of fresh ingredients, Australia is in the process of evolving its own unique food style. Your tastebuds should count their culinary blessings.—H.B.

Soups

Soups are never served as a first course in Thailand, but are part of the shared meal, their role being to cleanse and refresh the palate between courses. It's almost unthinkable for Thais to have a meal without some sort of soup on the table. On a recent food tour in Bangkok, after ordering an extensive selection of dishes, the waitress asked, 'No soup?' It was puzzling to her that we would have all this food but no soup to revive our palate between the different dishes. Like Thai food generally, Thai soups are infinite in their variety.—A.F.

Hot and Sour Soup with Prawns, Oyster Mushrooms and Young Coconut

Serves 4 or 8 as part of a selection of dishes

Tom Yum-style soups are the best known Thai soups, with Tom Yum Goong (prawns/shrimp) one of the most popular. The following recipe has coconut milk and young coconut flesh. Until a few years ago, I had no idea that Tom Yum soup could be enriched with coconut milk. We enjoyed this version at Chot Chit, a tiny royal Thai restaurant in the old section of Bangkok. There it would be considered sacrilege to use good quality prawns and not leave the head and shell on, but you can decide whether or not to peel. Feel free to omit the coconut milk, and any meat, seafood or vegetables can be used instead of the prawns.

3 cups (750ml/26 fl oz) chicken stock (see page 124)
2 stalks lemongrass, bruised and cut into 5cm (2 in) pieces
5 thin slices of galangal
10 kaffir lime leaves
2 tablespoons roasted chilli paste
2 small chillies, thinly sliced
1 tomato, cut into wedges
75ml (2½ fl oz/¹/3 cup) fish sauce

8 large green prawns (shrimp), still with head and shell, slit down the middle and vein removed
150gm (5 oz) oyster mushrooms, in bite-sized pieces
125ml (4 fl oz/½ cup) lime juice
¹/3 cup (80ml/2½ fl oz) coconut milk
½ cup young coconut flesh (omit if unavailable)
¼ cup coriander (cilantro) leaves and stem, roughly chopped

Bring the chicken stock to boil, add the lemongrass, galangal and kaffir lime leaves. Simmer a few minutes and add the chilli paste, chillies, tomato and fish sauce. Bring to a simmer and add the prawns. When the prawns are just starting to cook, stir in the lime juice, coconut milk and coconut flesh. Remove from heat as soon as the prawns have cooked and stir in the coriander leaves and stem.

Divide between serving bowls or pour into a large soup bowl if sharing. Serve with a finger bowl if prawns are left unpeeled.

Chicken and Rice Noodle Soup from Siam Square

Serves 4

This type of noodle soup is fast food and is not shared, but is a one-bowl meal. A few years ago I had this version from a vendor in Siam Square and it came with a big plate of fresh herbs and condiments, a very generous portion of noodles and a broth flavoured with cassia and cinnamon. Any type of noodle can be used.

3 cups (750ml/26 fl oz) chicken stock (see page 124)
2 tablespoons sweet soy sauce
2 tablespoons soy sauce
1 tablespoon ginger, peeled and shredded
2 star anise
1 x 2½ cm (1 in) piece of cassia bark
4 chicken legs, trimmed
200g (7 oz) dried rice noodles, soaked in hot water until softened
2 green spring onions, including some of the green tops, thinly sliced
a few sprigs of coriander (cilantro)
a few sprigs of Thai basil
a few sprigs of mint
4 lime wedges
1 cup bean sprouts
2 tablespoons fish sauce
2–6 small red and green chillies, sliced

In a large saucepan bring the chicken stock to boil, add the soy sauces, ginger, star anise, cassia bark and chicken legs. Reduce to a simmer and cook until the chicken is tender, about 30–40 minutes. Divide the noodles between the serving bowls, then add the chicken and broth. Sprinkle with the green spring onions.

Arrange the herbs, lime wedges and bean sprouts on a plate. In a small bowl combine the fish sauce and red and green chillies and serve with the soup alongside the herb plate.

Spicy Mussel Soup with Ginger and Pineapple

Serves 4 or 8 as part of a selection of dishes

Fruit is used in all aspects of Thai cooking and is often combined with meat or seafood. The sweet tartness of the pineapple complements the richness of the mussels.

1 kg (2.2 lb) black mussels
2 red chillies, chopped
1 tablespoon coriander (cilantro) root, chopped
3 cloves garlic, peeled
1 tablespoon vegetable oil
3 cups (750ml/26 fl oz) chicken stock (see page 124)
1 tablespoon light palm sugar
2 tablespoons fish sauce
2 tablespoons oyster sauce
2 stalks lemongrass, bruised and cut into 5cm (2 in) pieces
2 tablespoons ginger, peeled and finely shredded
8 kaffir lime leaves
1 cup fresh pineapple, peeled and sliced
¼ cup chopped coriander (cilantro) leaves and stem

Wash the mussels and remove the beards if necessary.

In a mortar and using a pestle make a paste with the chillies, coriander root and garlic. Heat the oil in a wok or large pot and gently fry the paste. Add the stock, palm sugar, fish sauce, oyster sauce, lemongrass, ginger, kaffir lime leaves and pineapple. Bring to the boil and add the mussels. Cover with a tight-fitting lid and steam over high heat, shaking often, until mussels have opened (about 3–5 minutes). Sprinkle with coriander leaves and stem.

Divide mussels between serving bowls and spoon the broth over, or serve in a large bowl if sharing.

Chicken Stock

Makes about 2 litres (4 pints)

A good soup demands a good stock and stock is not hard to make. It can take time, but once it's simmering it doesn't take much more labour. Simple rules for stock: wash the bones well, start from cold water, skim often, bring up to the boil but never let boil. If allowed to boil, the scum emulsifies into the stock and it becomes cloudy and bitter. Your chicken stock should just be ticking over and be sparkling clear. Make in large quantities and, when cooked, strain, discarding the bones and vegetables. Cool completely in the fridge and then remove the fat from the top. Stock will freeze well for months.

2kg (4.4 lb) chicken bones
3 L (6 pints/12 cups) cold water
small knob ginger, peeled and sliced
3 washed coriander (cilantro) roots
4 unpeeled cloves garlic
1 peeled onion, sliced
2 cups celery, roughly chopped
½ teaspoon white pepper

Place chicken in a large pot and wash well in several changes of water. Add remaining ingredients and bring to the boil, skimming often. As soon as it looks like boiling, turn down to a very low simmer and cook for 2–3 hours, skimming well during the cooking time.

Taste ... Don't Measure!

One of the most overlooked measuring tools is your tongue.

Writing recipes is actually quite hard, because what is too much salt or sugar for one person is too little for another. In our classes, we find the occasional student who painstakingly measures every ingredient. But professional chefs often modify recipes dramatically just by tasting as they go.

Most Westerners' introduction to cooking is as a child, baking cakes and cookies where exact measurements are crucial. That's because baking is a science, based on chemistry. But Thai food is more art than science, where you express yourself through myriad flavours.

So let your tongue be your guide as you cook. And don't fear making mistakes ... taste and adjust a little, then taste and adjust some more.—A.F.

Chicken, Shiitake Mushroom and Omelette Soup

Serves 4 or 8 as part of a selection of dishes

The most common soups in a traditional Thai context are usually very simple, because they are meant to refresh the palate between more highly seasoned dishes. This usually doesn't work for a Western market because we tend to eat the soup first, as a stand-alone dish. The following recipe is from a repertoire known as gaeng jeut, which literally translates as 'bland liquid'. Not a great menu description but I personally don't find them bland; rather, they are delicate and subtle. A nice alternative to the omelette would be sliced silken tofu, and any mushrooms can be used.

½ cup (125ml/4 fl oz) vegetable oil
2 golden shallots, peeled and sliced thinly
2 eggs, lightly scrambled with a tablespoon of water
4 cups (1 L/34 fl oz) chicken stock (see opposite page)
4 chicken legs
4 dried shiitake mushrooms, soaked in boiling water until soft, then drained and thinly sliced
2 tablespoons light soy sauce
1 teaspoon oyster sauce
pinch of white sugar
¼ cup Thai basil leaves

Heat the vegetable oil to medium in a wok and deep-fry the shallots until golden. Drain on paper towel and set aside. Drain the oil from the wok and set aside (it can be used again for general cooking). Place the wok back on the burner and heat to almost smoking. Pour in the egg and tilt the wok to make a thin omelette. Remove from the wok and, when cool, cut into thin strips.

Place the chicken stock in a pot and bring to the boil. Add the chicken legs, mushrooms, soy sauce, oyster sauce and sugar. Simmer until the chicken is cooked, about 30 minutes. Remove the chicken from the stock and shred the meat. Add chicken back into the stock with the omelette and stir in the basil leaves.

Divide between serving bowls, or one large bowl if sharing, and sprinkle with the deep-fried shallots.

Curries

The word curry is derived from the Tamil language; it means 'sauce' and, for many of us, our first experience with a curry is an anglicised version of an Indian curry made with commercial curry powder. So when we come across the almost infinite variety of Thai curries, many of them don't seem familiar. In Thai, curries are called gaeng and refer to any dish with a lot of liquid and a paste, so while some Thai curries may resemble the Indian-style curries, others may be more like a soup.

Broadly speaking, Thai curries can be divided into four styles: coconut curries, which are the best known; stock-based curries; sour curries; and stir-fry curries.

Most of us are familiar with red, green, massaman, yellow and penang coconut-based curries. Red curries are often made from a large dried red chilli that has an intense flavour and mild to medium heat level. Green curries are made using fresh green chillies, often a combination of a long, thin green chilli and a small green birdseye chilli. Both chillies are very fiery and these curries are usually stunningly hot. Massaman is also made using large dried red chillies and is usually mild to medium; sweet spices like cardamom, clove and cinnamon are also used. Yellow curry is an Indian-influenced curry that uses curry powder as well as large dried red chillies. This is usually one of the mildest curries. Penang curry also uses dried red chillies and is usually a medium heat. Originally from Malaysia, this popular curry is creamy, sweet, rich and finished off with peanuts.

Jungle curries seem to be the best known of all the stock-based curries. They originate in the northern jungles, as the name implies, and make use of whatever fresh ingredients are available. The paste rarely contains spices apart from pepper, and the curry is always scorchingly hot. It usually contains a variety of vegetables, green peppercorns, the very aromatic krachai ginger and holy basil. The small green birdseye chillies are most commonly used but fresh hot red chillies can be used as well.

Gaeng Som is a sour style of curry. The souring agent can be tamarind water; tamarind leaves, which have a taste like sorrel; or even tart vegetables like tomato. Any seafood can be used and teamed with whatever vegetables are on hand. Sour curries, like stock-based curries, are eaten everywhere on a day-to-day basis throughout villages, markets and homes in Thailand. Though not as complex or familiar as the fried coconut curries, they are one of my favourite curries because of their adaptability to what's on hand and, served with a bowl of rice, are immensely satisfying and healthy.

One of my favourite stir-fry curries uses a paste similar to a classic red but without the complexity. This paste, known as Phrik King, is a medium to hot curry that uses long, thin dried red chillies and the only spice used is white peppercorns. The result of this dry curry is hot, sweet and salty. A popular version found at market stalls throughout Thailand is made with pork and snake beans.

Seafood Dumplings in Green Curry with Dill and Wild Ginger

Serves 6–8 as part of a selection of dishes

Green curry is always one of the most popular of the coconut curries. This curry can be simplified by using sliced seafood, though I think making the dumplings is worthwhile for a more impressive dish. I love using Atlantic salmon for this, although any fish can be used as long as it's not too muddy flavoured.

When I was travelling in north-eastern Thailand a few years ago, I became aware of the use of dill in Thai cuisine and have since come across dill frequently used with fish or sometimes in stock-based curries. Thai food is never predictable and often surprising.

Seafood Dumplings
6 white peppercorns
1 teaspoon coriander (cilantro) root, washed and scraped
1 clove of garlic
1 teaspoon ginger, peeled and roughly diced
250g (8 oz) boneless fish fillets, diced
125g (4 oz) green prawn (shrimp) meat, finely chopped
1 tablespoon rice or corn flour
1 tablespoon fish sauce
1 tablespoon thin soy sauce
pinch of white sugar

Curry
500ml (16 fl oz) coconut milk
2 tablespoons vegetable oil
3–4 tablespoons green curry paste (see page 13)
2 tablespoons fish sauce
1 tablespoon palm sugar
8 kaffir lime leaves
2 tablespoons dill, coarsely chopped
½ cup Thai basil leaves
1 tablespoon wild ginger (krachai), shredded

To make dumplings: Grind the peppercorns in a mortar and then add the coriander root, garlic and ginger. Pound to a paste. Place the fish in a food processor and pulse to a rough paste. (The longer the fish is in the food processor the more bouncy the texture as the protein strands are stretched). Transfer fish to a bowl and add the garlic and coriander paste, prawn meat, rice or corn flour, fish sauce, soy sauce and sugar. Mix well to combine and then with wet hands roll into 4cm (1½ in) dumplings. Bring a large pot of salted water to the boil and poach the dumplings. They are ready when they rise to the top. This should take about 4–5 minutes. Remove with a slotted spoon and drain on a tea towel.

To make curry: Open the tin of coconut milk without shaking and remove the thick cream from the top. Place in a wok or saucepan with the vegetable oil and simmer until the mixture looks curdled. Add the green curry paste and cook, stirring over a low heat until the paste smells fragrant. Add the remaining coconut milk, fish sauce, palm sugar and kaffir lime leaves. Bring to the boil then reduce heat to a simmer, add the poached seafood dumplings and cook a minute or so to warm through. Stir in the dill, basil and wild ginger, cook just until the basil has wilted and remove from heat. Transfer to a serving bowl.

Pork Curry with Water Spinach, Kaffir Lime and Tamarind

Serves 4 or 6–8 as part of a selection of dishes

This is a very easy and light style of red curry. Use baby spinach or Asian greens if water spinach is unavailable. Kaffir lime juice, with its intense perfume, is traditionally used to finish but ordinary limes will be fine.

3 tablespoons vegetable oil
3 cloves garlic, peeled and finely sliced
2 tablespoons red curry paste (see page 13)
250ml (8 fl oz) coconut milk
400g (14 oz) pork fillet, cut into strips
8 kaffir lime leaves
2 tablespoons fish sauce
2 tablespoons soy sauce
2 tablespoons tamarind water
1 tablespoon light palm sugar
250ml (8 fl oz) chicken stock (see page 124) or water
125g (4 oz) water spinach, English spinach or other leafy green
lime juice to taste

Heat the oil to moderate and fry the garlic, taking care not to burn it. Add the curry paste and fry until fragrant. Add the coconut milk and bring to the boil. Reduce to a simmer and add the pork fillet, lime leaves, fish sauce, soy sauce, tamarind water and palm sugar. Allow to simmer, stirring until the pork has cooked. This will only take a few minutes. Add the chicken stock and water spinach and simmer a further few minutes until the spinach has wilted. Add a squeeze of lime juice to taste and transfer to a serving bowl.

Penang Curry with Braised Beef Shin, Green Peppercorns and Basil

Serves 6–8 as part of a selection of dishes

This is another very popular and rich coconut curry that is usually offered at your local Thai restaurant with a choice of chicken, pork, beef or seafood. It is usually done with braised beef, as in Thailand the meat is often quite tough and needs long, slow cooking to tenderise it.

The beef shin used in this recipe may be more familiar as gravy beef. It takes a few hours to cook but, when ready, has a deliciously rich sticky texture, like lamb shanks. Other stewing cuts like chuck or brisket are also suitable. Green peppercorns are difficult to obtain fresh, but the imported pickled peppercorns are a good substitute—just rinse off the brine before using.

2 cups (500ml/17 fl oz) coconut cream
500g (1 lb) diced beef shin
2–3 tablespoons red curry paste (see page 13)
1–2 tablespoons light palm sugar
1–2 tablespoons fish sauce
4 tablespoons roasted crushed peanuts
2 teaspoons green peppercorns
8 kaffir lime leaves
½ cup basil leaves
1 large red chilli, de-seeded (pitted) and sliced

Open the coconut cream without shaking the tin and separate the cream from the milk. There should be about 1¼ cups of milk and ³/4 cup of cream. Place the diced beef in a pot with the coconut milk and just enough water to cover if necessary. Bring to the boil and simmer on a low heat uncovered until the meat is cooked. This takes about 2 hours. Let the meat cool in the liquid.

Heat ½ cup (125ml/4 fl oz) of the reserved coconut cream in a wok and simmer until the oil starts to separate. Add the curry paste and gently fry for about 5 minutes. Add the palm sugar, fish sauce, half of the peanuts, the braised beef and enough of the cooking liquid to make a thick sauce. Simmer on a low heat for 10–15 minutes, stirring occasionally. Lastly, stir in the peppercorns, kaffir lime leaves, basil leaves and chillies. Remove from heat as soon as the basil wilts. Transfer to a serving bowl and garnish with the remaining coconut cream and peanuts.

Green Curry of Braised Chicken, Bamboo Shoots, Ginger and Baby Corn

Serves 4 or 6–8 as part of a selection of dishes

Another family favourite, but I like to use chicken pieces on the bone instead of chicken strips. Cooking anything on the bone gives more flavour to the dish, but feel free to simplify with boneless chicken, either breast or thigh, and use whatever vegetables are on hand.

500ml (16 fl oz) coconut milk
2 tablespoons vegetable oil
3–4 tablespoons green curry paste (see page 13)
4 skinless chicken maryland, cut at the joint and cut in half again
2 tablespoons fish sauce
1 tablespoon light palm sugar
250ml (8 fl oz/1 cup) chicken stock (see page 124) or water
2 tablespoons tamarind water
2 tablespoons ginger, peeled and shredded
115g (3½ oz) punnet of baby corn, cut in half lengthways
½ cup bamboo shoots
4 double kaffir lime leaves
½ cup basil leaves
a few sprigs of coriander (cilantro) for garnish

Open the coconut milk without shaking the tin and remove the thick cream from the top. Combine in a wok or saucepan with the vegetable oil and cook until the mixture looks slightly curdled. Add the curry paste and fry on a low heat until the paste is fragrant. Add the chicken and stir to coat with the paste. Add the fish sauce, palm sugar, remaining coconut milk and stock. Bring to the boil and simmer uncovered until the chicken is cooked. This will take about 20–30 minutes. Add the tamarind water, ginger, baby corn and bamboo shoots, cook for another 5 minutes and then finish with the kaffir lime leaves and basil leaves. Transfer to a serving bowl and garnish with coriander.

Southern Style Chicken Curry with Turmeric and Potatoes

Serves 4 or 6–8 as part of a selection of dishes

The name of this dish, Gai Kolae, refers to the fishing boats found in the waters of southern Thailand. Like the boats, it has a vibrant colour from the fresh turmeric and fresh red and green chillies.

Curry Paste
5 large dried chillies, de-seeded (pitted) and soaked in hot water for 10 minutes
pinch of salt
1 teaspoon fresh turmeric, peeled and roughly chopped
1 teaspoon coriander (cilantro) seeds, roasted and ground
1 teaspoon cumin seeds, roasted and ground
1 teaspoon roasted shrimp paste

Curry
4 tablespoons vegetable oil
4 skinless chicken maryland, cut at the joint and cut in half again
1 tablespoon garlic, roughly chopped
500ml (16 fl oz) coconut milk
250ml (8 fl oz) chicken stock (see page 124) or water
4 tablespoons fish sauce
2 tablespoons light palm sugar
300g (11 oz) peeled waxy potatoes, cut into chunks
1 large red chilli, de-seeded (pitted) and sliced
1 large green chilli, de-seeded (pitted) and sliced
lime juice to taste
coriander (cilantro) sprigs to garnish

To make curry paste: Finely chop the chillies, add to a mortar with the remaining ingredients and pound to a smooth paste with a pestle.

To make curry: Heat the oil in a wok or saucepan and fry the chicken pieces until golden. Remove and then fry the garlic on a moderate heat until starting to colour. Add all the curry paste and fry gently until fragrant.

Add the coconut milk, stock, chicken, fish sauce and palm sugar. Bring to the boil then simmer for 15–20 minutes.

Add the potatoes and simmer until tender. Finish with the lime juice and chillies, transfer to a serving bowl and garnish with the coriander.

Massaman of Duck with Sweet Potato and Cashews

Serves 6–8 as part of a selection of dishes

Massaman is most commonly made with stewing beef or chicken with potatoes. With its rich flavour, duck works well with the spices, and a starchy vegetable like sweet potato complements the dish perfectly.
A lot of home cooks are intimidated by using duck, so I suggest you just buy the maryland cut for this dish. This recipe may seem convoluted but the end result is worth the work. You can use stewing meat such as beef shin, chuck steak or a chicken maryland cut. Follow the same technique, but adjust the braising time for the different meats.

4 duck maryland, jointed and drumstick trimmed
3 cups (750ml/26 fl oz) coconut cream
4 tablespoons vegetable oil
6–8 pickling onions or golden shallots, peeled
500g (1 lb) golden sweet potato, peeled and cut
5cm (2 in) pieces
3–4 tablespoons Massaman paste (see page 14)

2–3 tablespoons light palm sugar
2–3 tablespoons fish sauce
4 tablespoons tamarind water
1 large red chilli, de-seeded (pitted) and sliced
¼ cup roasted unsalted cashews, roughly chopped

Heat a heavy-based frypan and cook the duck pieces until well coloured. Set aside.

Open the coconut cream without shaking and separate the cream from the milk. There should be about 1 cup (250ml/8 fl oz) of cream and 2 cups (500ml/17 fl oz) of milk. Place the milk in a saucepan with the duck pieces, adding just enough water to cover if necessary. Set the coconut cream aside to use later. Bring the duck to the boil without covering, and then simmer on a low heat for about 1½–2 hours. The duck can also be placed in a baking dish with the coconut milk and cooked uncovered in a moderately low oven (160°C/325°F/Gas Mark 3).

Meanwhile, place the sweet potato and onions in a baking dish with the vegetable oil, toss well to coat and bake in a moderate oven (180°C/350°F/Gas Mark 4) for about an hour or until browning on the edges and cooked. Remove and set aside.

Once the duck is cooked, remove from coconut milk and reserve milk.

Heat half of the reserved coconut cream in a wok or saucepan and simmer for about 5–10 minutes, until the oil starts to separate. Add the massaman paste and cook gently until the paste smells rich and fragrant. Add the reserved coconut milk, light palm sugar, fish sauce and tamarind water. Bring to the boil, then add the cooked duck pieces, sweet potato, onion and half of the remaining coconut cream. Simmer for another 15 minutes, stirring occasionally. Transfer to a serving bowl and garnish with the red chilli, cashews and remaining coconut cream.

Chiang Mai Pork Curry
with Pickled Garlic

Serves 6–8 as part of a selection of dishes

One of the highlights of our food tour in Bangkok is dining at Face Restaurant—a beautiful modern Thai restaurant built in the style of a traditional Thai teak house linked with verandahs and water features. A popular curry on the menu is Gaeng Hang Lae or Northern style pork curry. It's said to have originated in Burma, with the Thais adapting it during the time they were under Burmese rule, between the 16th and 18th centuries.

During our adventures in the food markets of Bangkok, we always come across a bewildering array of pickles, which can be used as a condiment or as part of a dish. A lot of simple vinegar and sugar pickles are made at home, while the more complex salty styles are left to the experts and bought from the markets. Pickled garlic tastes like a cross between sweet-and-sour pickled onion and roast garlic. Make your own (see page 23) or buy jars from any big Asian supermarket.

4 cloves garlic

1 tablespoon fresh turmeric

4 tablespoons vegetable oil

3–4 tablespoons red curry paste (see page 13)

500g (1 lb) pork neck or belly cut into 2½ cm (1 in) pieces

400ml (14 oz) coconut cream

½ cup (125ml/4 fl oz) chicken stock (see page 124)

1 head pickled garlic, peeled (see page 23)

2 tablespoons pickled garlic syrup

¼ cup ginger, peeled and shredded

3–4 tablespoons fish sauce

2–3 tablespoons palm sugar

2–3 tablespoons tamarind water

3 star anise

5cm (2 in) piece of cassia bark

½ cup roasted unsalted peanuts

In a mortar and pestle, make a paste with the garlic and turmeric.

Heat the oil in a saucepan or wok and gently fry the garlic and turmeric paste for 1 minute. Add the curry paste and fry another 5 minutes on low heat, stirring constantly. Add the pork and stir-fry a few more minutes to coat with the paste. Add the remaining ingredients, bring to the boil and then reduce to a simmer until the meat is tender, about 1 to 1½ hours. Taste and adjust the seasoning; it should be creamy, sweet and salty with a little tartness from the tamarind. Serve with steamed rice.

Issan-Style Chicken, Pumpkin and Dill Curry

Serves 4 or 6–8 as part of a selection of dishes

There's a province just a few hours north-east of Bangkok, called Pak Chong. It's a major agricultural area with many farms following the King's organic farming methods and there are even a few wineries. It was here, in a popular restaurant built as a series of decks overlooking a scenic lake, that I enjoyed this simple stock-based curry. The waitress said it was very hot and even after requesting it not too hot, it was fiery. I have taken the heat level down quite a few notches in this recipe and it can be adapted to suit whatever vegetables and meat are on hand.

It's the liberal use of dill and roasted rice powder that give this curry its distinctive Issan (north-eastern) flavour.

Paste

2 large red chillies, de-seeded (pitted) and chopped
2–8 small red chillies, chopped
2 golden shallots, peeled and diced
4 cloves garlic, peeled
1 tablespoon galangal, peeled and chopped
2 stalks lemongrass, bottom half only, outer leaves removed and finely diced
pinch of salt

Curry

2 cups (500ml/17 fl oz) chicken stock (see page 124)
all of the above paste
400g (14 oz) chicken thigh or breast meat cut into stir-frying strips

2 cups peeled pumpkin, cut into 2½ cm (1 in) dice
2 long Thai or Japanese eggplants (aubergines), cut in half lengthways then into 2½ cm (1 in) pieces
2 tablespoons roasted rice powder
1 cup snake or green beans, trimmed and cut into 2½ cm (1 in) pieces
2–3 tablespoons fish sauce
1–2 teaspoons white sugar
½ cup dill
½ cup basil
4 green spring onions, cut into 2½ cm (1 in) pieces
10 kaffir lime leaves

To make paste: Combine all ingredients in a mortar and pound to a paste.

To make curry: Bring stock to the boil and add the paste, reduce to a simmer and cook a few minutes. Add the chicken, pumpkin, eggplant and roasted rice powder. When the pumpkin and eggplant are almost cooked, add the beans and simmer a few minutes. Add the fish sauce, sugar, dill, basil, green spring onions and kaffir lime leaves. Simmer a few more minutes, then transfer to a serving bowl.

Steamed Red Curry with Prawns and Pumpkin

Serves 4–8 as part of a selection of dishes

Hor Mok Pla is a steamed fish curry that can often be found at curry vendors throughout Thailand. I like to do an elegant version in the class, where we line a bamboo steamer basket with banana leaves, add a layer of basil, a layer of seafood and then pour the curry sauce over the seafood before gently steaming. The basket is placed on the table with the other dishes and shared. It's a sublime, delicate and creamy curry—perfect for an impressive Thai dinner party. The following version uses the combination of prawns (shrimp) and pumpkin but you could also use a mix of seafood, or omit the pumpkin altogether. Like so many recipes, this is about the technique.

If you don't have banana leaves on hand, baking paper is fine; and another alternative is just to steam the dish in a glass or porcelain bowl. It could also be divided between small bowls and served as an entree or starter. The steaming time will vary slightly depending on the size of the basket or bowl.

Curry Sauce
2 cups (500ml/17 fl oz) coconut cream
1 tablespoon light palm sugar
2 tablespoons fish sauce
2 eggs, lightly beaten
2–3 tablespoons red curry paste (see page 13)

Curry
1 cup basil leaves
16 large green prawns (shrimp), peeled, de-veined, heads and tails removed
2 cups Kent pumpkin, peeled, cut into 5cm (2 in) pieces and lightly steamed
8 kaffir lime leaves, finely shredded
curry sauce
½ large red chilli, de-seeded (pitted) and cut into fine shreds
handful of coriander (cilantro) leaves for garnish

To make curry sauce: Open the coconut cream without shaking it and remove thick cream from the top. Reserve cream for garnish. Combine the palm sugar and fish sauce in a bowl, stir to dissolve palm sugar, add the eggs, curry paste and coconut cream.

To make curry: Line a medium steamer basket with banana leaves or baking paper. Layer over the basil leaves, then the prawns and pumpkin. Sprinkle over half the shredded kaffir lime leaves and then the curry sauce. Place basket over a wok filled with boiling water. Cover and steam over a moderate heat for about 15–20 minutes. Remove from heat and place basket on a serving plate. Swirl over reserved coconut cream, reserved kaffir lime leaves, chilli strips and coriander leaves.

Sour Curry of Prawns, Snake Beans and White Radish with Steamed Savoury Custard

Serves 4–8 as part of a selection of dishes

Sour Curry

4 cups (1 L/34 fl oz) chicken stock (see page 124)
curry paste (use paste from Sour Curry with Crispy Fish, Cherry Tomatoes and Spinach recipe, see page 147)
4 tablespoons tamarind water
2–3 tablespoons fish sauce
1–2 tablespoons light palm sugar
1 cup white radish, peeled and cut into
5cm (2 in) x 1cm (½ in) pieces
16 large green prawns (shrimp), peeled and de-veined
1 cup snake or green beans, topped, tailed and sliced into 2½ cm (1 in) pieces
1 tomato, cut into thin wedges
handful of coriander (cilantro) sprigs

Steamed Savoury Custard

3 eggs
1 tablespoon fish sauce
pinch of white sugar
1 green spring onion, trimmed and thinly sliced, including some of the green top
2 tablespoons water
2 tablespoons coconut cream
freshly ground white pepper
small handful of chopped coriander (cilantro) leaves

To make curry: Bring the chicken stock to boil in a wok or saucepan and add all the curry paste. Simmer a few minutes before adding the tamarind water, fish sauce and palm sugar. Simmer until sugar has dissolved and add the white radish, cook a few minutes until just starting to soften. Then add the prawns and snake beans. Simmer until the prawns are just starting to lose translucency, then add the tomato and cook for only another minute or until prawns are ready. Remove from heat and transfer to a serving bowl. Garnish with coriander sprigs.

To make steamed custard: Whisk eggs then add the fish sauce, sugar, spring onion, water and coconut cream, stirring to combine. Pour into a heatproof bowl and steam over gently simmering water until just cooked. This takes about 15 minutes, depending on the depth of the bowl. Season with white pepper and coriander leaves. Serve from the bowl.

Lemongrass Chicken Curry

Serves 4 or 6–8 as part of a selection of dishes

One of the FAQs at the cooking classes is about lemongrass and how to use it. This recipe illustrates the two ways lemongrass is used. The very tender inner core is used in the curry paste, while pieces of the whole plant are used in the final dish to impart the delicate citrus notes—but are then discarded.

Lemongrass is high in vitamin A and medicinally is considered good for headaches and for stimulating the appetite. It is very easy to grow, sometimes a little too easy as it can form a very large clump, but having some in the garden certainly makes for very fresh Thai cooking. Don't even consider using the processed stuff in a jar.

Curry Paste
1 stalk lemongrass, bottom half only, outer leaves removed then finely chopped
1 tablespoon galangal, peeled and chopped
2 teaspoons lime zest
2 golden shallots, peeled and chopped
4 coriander (cilantro) roots, washed and chopped
4 cloves garlic, peeled
4 large dried chillies, de-seeded (pitted) and soaked in hot water until soft, then coarsely chopped
1 teaspoon roasted shrimp paste
2 teaspoons fresh turmeric, peeled and chopped
pinch of salt

Curry
3 tablespoons vegetable oil
all of the above paste
400g (14 oz) chicken thigh fillet cut into 5cm (2 in) pieces
4 tablespoons fish sauce
1 cup (250ml/8 fl oz) chicken stock (see page 124)
2 teaspoons light palm sugar
2 stalks lemongrass, outer leaves removed, bruised lightly and cut into 7cm (3 in) pieces
12 kaffir lime leaves
lime juice to taste (kaffir lime juice if available)

To make paste: Place all ingredients in a mortar and pound to a paste. Any leftover paste will keep refrigerated for 2–3 weeks, or freeze in ice cube trays.

To make curry: Heat the oil in a wok or pot and cook half the paste over a moderate heat for a few minutes until fragrant. Add the chicken and stir-fry to coat with the paste and seal well. Add the fish sauce, chicken stock, palm sugar, lemongrass and kaffir lime leaves. Lower the heat and gently simmer for 10 minutes or until the chicken has cooked. Season to taste with the lime juice and then transfer to a serving plate.

Jungle Curry with Moo Grob

Serves 4 or 6–8 as part of a selection of dishes

This recipe uses Moo Grob or crispy pork, which is rather indulgent, but the more everyday pork or chicken could always be substituted.

Jungle Curry Paste
¼ teaspoon white peppercorns
2 large green chillies, de-seeded (pitted) and chopped
6–10 small green chillies, chopped
1 tablespoon galangal, peeled and chopped
2 stalks lemongrass, bottom half only, outer leaves removed, then finely chopped
1 tablespoon wild ginger or krachai, chopped
2 golden shallots, peeled and chopped
6 cloves garlic, peeled and chopped
pinch of salt

Curry
3 tablespoons vegetable oil
all of the above paste
2 cups (500ml/17 fl oz) chicken stock (see page 124) or water
2–3 tablespoons fish sauce
1 teaspoon white sugar
1 cup snake or green beans
1 cup baby corn, cut in half
½ cup bamboo shoots
2 tablespoons wild ginger or krachai, shredded
10 kaffir lime leaves
300g (11 oz) sliced Moo Grob (see page 45)
1 tablespoon green peppercorns
1 cup basil leaves

To make paste: Grind the peppercorns in a mortar, then add remaining ingredients and pound to a paste.

To make curry: Heat the oil in a wok or saucepan and gently fry the paste for a few minutes. Add the stock, fish sauce and sugar. Bring to the boil then reduce to a simmer, adding the beans, baby corn, bamboo shoots, wild ginger and kaffir lime leaves. Simmer for a few minutes then add the Moo Grob, peppercorns and basil leaves. Remove from heat as soon as the basil wilts. Transfer to a serving bowl.

Steamed Curry with Mushrooms, Sweet Potato and Tofu

Serves 4–8 as part of a selection of dishes

In Laos, they do a similar dish to the Thai Hor Mok but it's called Amok and I've had the best, and worst, of this dish in Vientiane. The worst was a steamed fish curry full of bones, skin and made with cheap muddy river fish, but the best was this simple vegetarian Amok made with mushrooms, sweet potato and tofu at the delightful Makphet restaurant. Just about any combination of vegetables works well, but avoid any that overcook too quickly.

Curry Sauce
2 cups (500ml/17 fl oz) coconut cream
1 tablespoon light palm sugar
2 tablespoons soy sauce
2 eggs, lightly beaten
2–3 tablespoons red curry paste (see page 13)

Curry
1 cup (250g/8 oz) basil leaves
2 cups (500g/1 lb) mixed mushrooms, washed and trimmed
2 cups (500g/1 lb) golden sweet potato, cut into 5cm (2 in) pieces and lightly steamed
250g (1 lb) firm tofu, cut into 1cm (½ in) dice
8 kaffir lime leaves, finely shredded
curry sauce
½ large red chilli, de-seeded (pitted) and finely shredded
handful of coriander (cilantro) leaves

To make curry sauce: Open coconut cream without shaking and remove cream from the top. Reserve cream to use as garnish. Dissolve the palm sugar with the soy sauce, then add the eggs, remaining coconut cream and curry paste.

To make curry: Line a medium steamer basket with banana leaves or baking paper, layer over the basil, then the mushrooms, sweet potato and tofu, sprinkle over half the kaffir lime leaves then pour over the curry sauce. Place basket over a wok filled with boiling water. Cover and steam on a moderate heat until the curry sauce has set slightly. This takes about 15–20 minutes. Place steamer basket on a serving plate and garnish with the reserved coconut cream, kaffir lime leaves, red chilli and coriander (cilantro) leaves.

Sour Curry with Crispy Fish, Cherry Tomatoes and Spinach

Serves 4 or 8 as part of a selection of dishes

This style of curry is very common and easy to make. Any seafood and all sorts of vegetables can be used for this dish. Some of the more common vegetables are snake beans, cabbage, white radish, bamboo shoots and tomato. A popular dish to complement this curry is a delicate, creamy, steamed savoury egg custard or even just a simple omelette.

Curry Paste
4 large red dried chillies, de-seeded (pitted) and soaked in hot water for 10 minutes
2 small red dried chillies, de-seeded (pitted) and soaked in hot water for 10 minutes
1 tablespoon galangal, peeled and diced
¼ cup (60g/2 oz) golden shallots or onion, peeled and chopped
1 tablespoon dried prawns (shrimp), soaked in hot water for 10 minutes, then drained
2 teaspoons shrimp paste
pinch of salt

Curry
400g (14 oz) good quality fish fillets
rice or corn flour for dusting
2 cups (500ml/17 fl oz) vegetable oil for deep-frying
4 cups (1 L/34 fl oz) chicken stock (see page 124)
curry paste
4 tablespoons tamarind water
2–3 tablespoons fish sauce
1–2 tablespoons light palm sugar
100g (3½ oz) baby spinach leaves
200g (7 oz) punnet of cherry tomatoes, halved

To make curry paste: Chop chillies finely and combine with remaining ingredients in a mortar. Pound to a paste.

To make curry: Slice fish into thin medallions and dust with rice or corn flour. Heat oil to medium heat in a wok and fry fish in batches until golden and crispy. Drain on paper towel and keep warm in a low oven.

Heat the stock in a wok or saucepan. Once simmering, add the curry paste and cook for a few minutes. Add the tamarind water, fish sauce and palm sugar. When the palm sugar has dissolved, add the spinach leaves and tomatoes. Simmer until the spinach has just started to wilt and then lastly add the fish pieces. Transfer to a serving bowl.

Seafood

With a coastline of over 2000 kilometres and one of the world's largest fishing fleets, it's no wonder seafood is popular and plentiful in Thailand. We always visit a large wholesale seafood market in Bangkok during our food tours and the variety and freshness is astounding.

Whole Fish Grilled in Banana Leaf with Pickled Plum, Ginger and Spring Onions

Serves 4–6 as part of a selection of dishes

This is another dish that has its roots in China but has been adapted by the Thais. The pickled green plums are about the size of a cumquat and, despite the name, are actually a type of apricot. The best brands come from China and they impart a distinctive sour and salty note to the dish.

If banana leaves are unavailable, simply replace with baking paper.

1 whole fish about 600–700g (21–25 oz), cleaned
2 coriander (cilantro) roots, washed and scraped
2 green spring onions, white part sliced thinly, green part sliced thinly for garnish
4 pickled plums, pitted and roughly chopped
2 tablespoons pickled plum juice
1 tablespoon fish sauce
1 tablespoon light soy sauce
½ teaspoon white sugar
¼ cup ginger, peeled and finely shredded
handful of coriander (cilantro) leaves for garnish
1 large red chilli, de-seeded (pitted) and julienned for garnish

Make three diagonal slashes on the fish and put the coriander roots into its cavity. In a bowl, mix together the plums, pickled plum juice, fish sauce, soy sauce and sugar.

Place the fish on a banana leaf and spoon the combined sauce over the fish. Sprinkle the fish with the white part of the spring onion and the shredded ginger. Fold the banana leaf over and then wrap the package in aluminium foil.

Cook on a preheated barbecue (grill), turning a few times, for about 20 minutes.

Carefully open the foil package, taking care not to lose any of the cooking juices. Transfer the fish to a serving platter and pour over the reserved juices. Garnish with the reserved green spring onion, coriander leaves and red chillies.

Crispy Sardines with Mint, Ginger and Tamarind Dressing

Serves 4 or 8 as part of a selection of dishes

Other strong and oily fish like mackerel can be used for this dish. The use of red curry paste as a seasoning along with the tamarind dressing gives this dish its very Thai flavour.

400g (14 oz) fresh sardines
1–2 tablespoons red curry paste (see page 13)
2 cups (500ml/17 fl oz) vegetable oil
¼ cup mint leaves
¼ cup coriander (cilantro) leaves
3 tablespoons ginger, finely shredded
1 large red chilli, sliced

Mint, Ginger and Tamarind Dressing
3 tablespoons fish sauce
4 tablespoons thick tamarind water (see page 25)
4 tablespoons light palm sugar
2 tablespoons lime juice

Clean sardines by removing the head, slit along the belly and remove the guts and backbone. Wash and dry with paper towel and toss with the red curry paste. Leave to marinate for an hour. Heat oil in a wok and fry the sardines in batches until crispy and golden. This takes about 5–7 minutes. Drain on paper towel and toss with the dressing, mint and coriander leaves, ginger and chilli. Transfer to a serving plate.

To make the dressing: Combine the fish sauce, tamarind water and palm sugar in a saucepan and bring to the boil. Simmer a few minutes until the palm sugar has dissolved and the sauce has slightly thickened. Cool and then stir in the lime juice.

Barbecued Squid with Green Peppercorns and Basil

Serves 4 or 8 as part of a selection of dishes

The following recipe is simple and relies on using fresh squid or cuttlefish.

500 g (1 lb) squid, cleaned and scored
2 tablespoons oyster sauce
4 tablespoons coconut cream
1–2 tablespoons fresh or pickled green peppercorns, rinsed of brine
½ cup basil leaves
1 tablespoon fish sauce
squeeze of fresh lime juice
½ cup coriander (cilantro) leaves

Place the cleaned squid in a bowl with the oyster sauce and coconut cream. Marinate in the refrigerator for 1 hour.

Chargrill the squid on a medium heat until it curls and loses translucency. Transfer to a bowl and add the green peppercorns, basil leaves, fish sauce and lime juice. Toss well to combine and transfer to a serving platter. Garnish with the coriander leaves.

Steamed Scallops with Lime and Chilli

Serves 4 as an entree/starter, or 8 as part of a selection of dishes

One evening, on the way to Le Lys, a Bangkok restaurant, our taxi became stuck in a typical Bangkok gridlock. (The Thai name for traffic jam, rot dhit mak mak, always makes me laugh, because it translates as 'sticky traffic'.) We abandoned our cab and headed on foot down a quiet side street to the restaurant, which is on the bottom floor of the owner's house. Set back from the street in a leafy garden and owned by a Belgian expat and his Thai wife, it had the added attraction of a big selection of Belgian beers.

The menu was interesting, but the dish I remember the best was also the simplest: fresh clams steamed and served on a lettuce leaf with a slice of hot chilli, a squeeze of lime juice and a splash of fish sauce. In this interpretation, I have used scallops, but use fresh clams if they are available. Green prawns (shrimp) would also make a great substitute.

16 medium scallops
1 head of soft lettuce, such as green mignonette
2 tablespoons mint, finely shredded
6 kaffir lime leaves, finely shredded
2–3 medium–hot chillies, thinly sliced
lime juice
fish sauce

Line a bamboo steamer basket with banana leaf or baking paper and add scallops in one layer. Place basket over a wok full of rapidly boiling water and steam until just cooked. This will only take a minute or two. When the scallops are cooked, place each one on a piece of lettuce and add a sprinkle of mint leaves, a few shreds of lime leaves and a slice or two of hot chillies. Squeeze over some lime juice and a splash of fish sauce.

These are best eaten in one or two bites so as to enjoy the contrasting flavours.

Steamed Sesame and Ginger King Prawns

Serves 4, or 8 as part of a selection of dishes

This simple and quick dish relies on the quality of the seafood. I recommend spending the extra money and buying Australian wild caught prawns (shrimp) for the best result.

It would be unthinkable in Asia to serve such expensive seafood without the head. Along with the legs, the head has lots of flavour. Ironically, a lot of Westerners find the head off-putting, and wouldn't order the dish if the prawns weren't peeled and heads removed.

12 large king prawns (shrimp), peeled, de-veined but with tail and heads left on (optional)
2 tablespoons oyster sauce
2 tablespoons ginger, finely shredded
1 large green chilli, de-seeded (pitted) and julienned
2 green spring onions, finely sliced, including some of the green part
½ teaspoon ground white pepper
2 tablespoons soy sauce
2 tablespoons Shaoxing wine
2 tablespoons peanut oil
1 tablespoon sesame oil
¼ cup coriander (cilantro) leaves

Toss prawns with oyster sauce and place in a bamboo steamer basket lined with baking paper. Place basket over a wok of rapidly boiling water and steam, covered, for about 8–10 minutes or until just cooked.

Transfer to a serving plate and cover with the ginger, chilli, spring onions and pepper. Combine the soy sauce and Shaoxing wine and sprinkle over the prawns. In a small saucepan, combine the peanut and sesame oils. Heat until almost smoking, then pour over the prawns. Garnish with the coriander leaves before serving.

Steamed Mussels with Krachai and Basil

Serves 4 as an entree/starter, or 8 as part of a selection of dishes

Though common in Thai markets, krachai is rarely available fresh in Australia. It can be bought in Asian supermarkets pickled in a light brine solution. Just rinse before using.

1 kg (2.2 lb) live black mussels (clams), cleaned
¼ cup shredded krachai
½ cup Thai basil leaves

Dipping Sauce
2 cloves garlic, peeled
2 coriander (cilantro) roots, washed and chopped
2–6 small red and green chillies, chopped
¼ cup (60ml/2 fl oz) lime juice
3–4 tablespoons fish sauce
2–3 teaspoons white sugar

To prepare mussels: Place the mussels in a heavy-based pan and add the krachai, cover and steam over high heat for 3–4 minutes. Remove the lid and add the basil, tossing the mussels well, and cover again. Cook until the mussels have opened, about 5 minutes. Transfer to a large bowl, discarding any mussels that haven't opened. Serve with the sauce on the side for dipping.

To make sauce: Make a paste with the garlic, coriander roots and chillies. Transfer to a bowl and stir in the lime juice, fish sauce and white sugar.

Whole Crispy Fish with Roasted Chilli Paste and Lemongrass

Serves 6–8 as part of a selection of dishes

Whole crispy fish has been on the Spirit House restaurant menu since Day One. It has an amazing 'wow factor' when placed on the table and is almost the Spirit House signature dish. This dish is a good example of how Westerners sometimes misunderstand certain characteristics of Asian food—in this case it's the textural component. Crispy, bouncy, chewy, rubbery and sticky are not usually desirable characteristics in Western cooking, but they certainly play an important role in Asian food.

I will always remember my first complaint about the crispy fish: 'This fish is all dry and overcooked.' That's the point! The dish is not meant to be eaten on its own but as part of a selection of dishes to be shared and enjoyed for its chewy, crispy texture. The following recipe is based on a whole crispy fish we had riverside in the old Thai capital of Ayutthaya.

1 whole firm fleshed white fish about 750g (1.5 lb), scaled and gutted, for example red emperor or gold band snapper
4 cups (1 L/34 fl oz) vegetable oil

Sauce
2 stalks lemongrass, finely chopped, bottom half only and outer leaves removed
8 kaffir lime leaves

2 teaspoons light palm sugar
2 tablespoons fish sauce
2 tablespoons tamarind water
4 tablespoons roasted chilli paste
½ cup (125ml/4 fl oz) chicken stock (see page 124) or water
½ cup Thai basil leaves
1 large red chilli, de-seeded (pitted) and thinly sliced

Dry the fish well inside and out with paper towel. Crosshatch with deep diagonal cuts almost to the bone.

Heat the oil in a wok to medium high and carefully lower the fish into the oil. Take care initially, as it can splatter. Baste the fish with oil while cooking and after about 7–10 minutes carefully turn over and cook another 5 minutes. Remove from the wok and drain on paper towel.

Transfer to a serving plate and pour the prepared sauce over it.

To make sauce: Combine the lemongrass, kaffir lime leaves, palm sugar, fish sauce, tamarind water, roasted chilli paste and stock or water in a small saucepan and bring to the boil, stirring until the sugar has dissolved. Add the basil leaves and chilli. Remove from heat as soon as the basil has wilted.

Crispy Prawns With Garlic

Serves 4 as an entree/starter, or 8 as part of a selection of dishes

This classic Thai dish can also be done with fish fillets or squid. It's one of my favourites—the sauce is a perfect foil for the fried prawns (shrimp).

12 large green prawns (shrimp), peeled and de-veined
3 tablespoons corn or rice flour
3 cups (750ml/26 fl oz) vegetable oil for deep-frying
coriander (cilantro) leaves to garnish
lime wedges

Sauce
2 tablespoons vegetable oil
4 cloves garlic, peeled and thinly sliced
1 tablespoon ginger, peeled and grated
1 tablespoon soy sauce
1 tablespoon fish sauce
1 tablespoon coconut or rice vinegar
1 tablespoon white sugar
¼ cup (60ml/2 fl oz) water

Toss the prawns with the rice or corn flour. Heat the oil in a wok to almost smoking and deep-fry the prawns in batches until golden and crispy. Drain on paper towel and transfer to a serving platter. Drizzle with the sauce and sprinkle with the fried garlic. Garnish with coriander leaves and serve with the lime wedges.

To make sauce: Heat the vegetable oil to medium and fry the garlic until golden, remove and strain on paper towel. Add remaining ingredients to the oil and bring to the boil. Remove from heat.

Steamed Salmon with Spicy Black Bean and Ginger Paste

Serves 6

A lovely modern Asian dish using salmon that chef Katrina Ryan created for one of her seafood and salad classes. Any other good quality fish fillets would also be suitable.

6 x 150g (5 oz) portions salmon
1 large red chilli, de-seeded (pitted) and shredded thinly for garnish
coriander (cilantro) sprigs for garnish

Spicy Black Bean and Ginger Paste
2 tablespoons dried, salted black beans
90ml (3 fl oz) vegetable oil
2 tablespoons ginger, peeled and grated
4 cloves garlic, crushed
1 large red chilli, finely chopped
2 tablespoons sweet soy sauce
2 tablespoons palm sugar
1 teaspoon ground black pepper

Place the salmon on a plate that fits into a steamer basket. Divide the black bean paste between the salmon portions and steam, covered, for 6–7 minutes. Transfer to serving plates and garnish with the red chilli and coriander leaves.

To make paste: Soak the black beans in $^3/_4$ cup warm water for 10 minutes, then squeeze out water and chop the beans finely. Reserve the soaking water.

Heat vegetable oil and fry the ginger, garlic and chilli until soft and fragrant but not brown. Add the black beans, soy sauce, palm sugar and pepper and cook on a low heat until the sugar has dissolved. Moisten with some of the reserved black bean soaking water. The mixture should be liquid but thick.

Coconut Marinated Salmon

Serves 4–6 as an entree

This very elegant modern dish was inspired by a fabulous salmon entree I enjoyed at the Greyhound Cafe, a groovy cafe in the Paragon Centre in Bangkok. It's a favourite of our multi-talented tour guide, Acland Brierty, who hungers for their Caesar salad when the thought of another plate of rice is just too much. The cafe serves a mix of Western and modern Thai and is always packed with stylish young Thais, plus the Bangkok up-market 'ladies-who-lunch'. Sashimi-grade tuna or other quality fresh fish would work just as well as the salmon.

2 tablespoons coconut milk
2 teaspoons green curry paste (see page 13)
2 tablespoons lime juice
1 tablespoon fish sauce
1 teaspoon light palm sugar
350g (12½ oz) fresh salmon, thinly sliced
¼ cup bean sprouts to garnish
2 sprigs of coriander (cilantro) to garnish

Combine the coconut milk, green curry paste, lime juice, fish sauce and palm sugar. Spread the sliced salmon in one layer over a large serving platter. Pour the marinade over the fish and spread to coat well. Refrigerate for 2 hours. Delicious served with Chinese New Year Salad (see page 71).

Poultry

Chickens, ducks, quail—poultry is the cheapest and most readily available source of protein in Thailand. Every village has chickens running around the houses, ducks foraging in the rice paddies to keep down the insect pests, while wild birds and quail scurry in the undergrowth. In the village markets the poultry is still alive—but looking very nervous!

Melody's Roast Chicken Glazed with Tamarind and Kaffir Lime Leaf

Serves 4 or 8 as part of a picnic

This recipe comes from Melody Kemp who put together the itinerary for our fabulous food tour of Vientiane in Laos. Melody has lived for the past few decades in South-East Asia and her insights add an intriguing, politically astute, witty and sometimes appropriately cynical view of the behind-the-scenes workings of these various Asian countries. This was one of the many dishes that we have enjoyed during our picnic at Buddha Park on the banks of the Mekong, looking across the border from Laos towards Thailand.

1 size 16 chicken—1.6kg (2½ lb)
2 tablespoons galangal, peeled and roughly chopped
1 tablespoon ginger, peeled and roughly chopped
8 cloves garlic, peeled
2–3 large dried chillies, de-seeded (pitted) and soaked in hot water until soft, then finely chopped
¼ cup (60ml/2 fl oz) tamarind water
2 tablespoons light palm sugar
1 tablespoon fish sauce
1 tablespoon soy sauce
6 kaffir lime leaves
coriander (cilantro) leaves for garnish

Preheat oven to 180°C (350°F/Gas Mark 4).

Cut chicken into pieces and place in a large bowl.

Make a paste in a mortar with the galangal, ginger, garlic and dried chillies, then mix together with the tamarind water, palm sugar, fish sauce, soy sauce and kaffir lime leaves. Pour over the chicken, rubbing well to coat. Allow to marinate for 2 hours in the refrigerator. Bake in preheated oven for 45–60 minutes, turning occasionally, until chicken is cooked. Transfer to a serving plate and garnish with coriander leaves.

Red Braised Duck with Lychee and Ginger Salad

Serves 4 or 8 as part of a selection of dishes

Duck is the most popular main course on the Spirit House menu. Many home cooks are intimidated by it, but if you use the leg and thigh cuts, it's no harder than cooking a casserole. These cuts are sold as duck maryland and will be available from good butchers or supermarkets.

The technique of red braising is classically Chinese. The red refers to the glossy mahogany colour that the meat takes on from the soy sauces.

If you are a keen cook, the Chinese stock below is well worth making. In China, master stocks can be handed down within families as wedding presents—the stock can be generations old, continually boiled and added to, in readiness for the next use. Start this dish in the morning or the day before, as the stock needs to be chilled so the duck fat can be removed.

4 duck maryland
all of the master stock from recipe at right
2 green spring onions, including some of the green part, trimmed and thinly sliced
12 lychees, peeled, de-seeded (pitted) and halved
½ cup mint leaves
½ cup coriander (cilantro) leaves
½ red chilli, de-seeded (pitted) and finely shredded
2 tablespoons ginger, peeled and finely shredded
4 kaffir lime leaves, finely shredded
juice of half a lime

Master Stock
2 L (3½ pints) of water
250ml (8 fl oz) Shaoxing wine
125ml (4 fl oz) light soy sauce
75ml (2½ fl oz/^{1}/3 cup) dark soy sauce
100g (3½ oz) yellow rock sugar
2 pieces tangerine peel
2 pieces cassia bark
4 pieces star anise
1 knob ginger, roughly chopped
4 cloves garlic, peeled

To make master stock: Bring all the ingredients to boil in a large stock pot, simmer for half an hour. Strain. Makes about 2½ litres (4 pints). Any leftover master stock can be either refrigerated for up to a week or frozen for several months. Use as a base for soups, add a few spoonfuls to a stir-fry or use for braising meats.

To prepare duck: Preheat oven to 160°C (325°F/Gas Mark 3).

Trim excess fat from the duck and cut at the joint. Place in a baking dish, skin side down. Bring master stock to the boil in a saucepan and pour over the duck pieces so they are almost submerged. Cover with a lid or aluminium foil and place in oven. Cook for 1½ hours and then remove the lid or foil and turn ducks over to skin side up.

Cook for another hour until the meat is almost falling from the bone. Remove the duck from the stock and refrigerate until needed. Completely chill the master stock in the refrigerator and then remove the fat that will have set on top. Place stock in a saucepan, bring to the boil and reduce by half. The duck pieces can be either reheated in the reduced stock or, for crispy skin duck, placed in a shallow pan, skin side up with a little stock, then reheated uncovered in a 180°C (350°F/Gas Mark 4) oven.

While the duck is reheating and the sauce reducing, make the salad by combining the remaining ingredients in a bowl and tossing with a squeeze of lime juice.

Transfer duck pieces to serving bowl and pour over about ½ cup (125ml/4 fl oz) of reduced stock, then pile the lychee and ginger salad on top of the duck pieces.

Duck Braised with Ginger, Young Coconut Water and Lemongrass

Serves 4 or 8 as part of a selection of dishes

This dish shows its Vietnamese influence with the use of young coconut water. Thai food is well-known for its use of coconut milk, but Vietnamese recipes seldom use the milk, except in sweet snacks. Instead, the juice from young coconuts is often used for stewed dishes. Buy drinking coconuts from the supermarket, or tinned coconut water from Asian supermarkets. Otherwise, chicken stock can be used, but with the addition of an extra pinch of sugar.

4 duck maryland
4 spring onions, white part finely chopped, green part thinly sliced
2 cloves garlic, peeled and crushed
2 tablespoons ginger, peeled and grated
1/3 cup (80ml/2½ fl oz) fish sauce
2 tablespoons soy sauce
1 tablespoon light palm sugar
2 tablespoons vegetable oil
4 stalks lemongrass, outer leaves removed and cut into 5cm (2 in) pieces
2 cups (500ml/17 fl oz) young coconut water
2 cups (500ml/17 fl oz) chicken stock (see page 124)

Trim excess fat from duck and cut into the leg and thigh at the joint.

In a bowl, combine the white part of the spring onions, garlic, ginger, fish sauce, soy sauce and palm sugar. Place duck in a bowl and rub the marinade over the duck pieces. Marinate for 2 hours. Remove the duck from the marinade and dry on a paper towel.

Heat the oil in a frypan and brown the duck pieces. Transfer to a saucepan or pot and add reserved marinade, lemongrass, coconut water and stock. Bring to the boil, skimming well to remove impurities. Reduce to a low simmer and cook uncovered for 1½–2 hours, skimming well during the cooking time. Transfer duck to a serving bowl, ladle over some of the braising liquid, and garnish with the green spring onion.

Twice Cooked Chicken Wings with Five-Spice and Black Vinegar Caramel

Serves 6–8 as an occasional snack

These make just the best snack, but beware! They are very addictive and can only be eaten on the odd occasion. They are closely related to twice-cooked pork belly and neither will ever make it onto the Weight Watchers program. But like most things in life, moderation is the key and a little every now and then will be good for you. It's best to start preparation the day before, as the drier the wings, the crispier the end result.

1 kg (2.2 lb) chicken wings
2½ L (4 pints) master stock (see page 175)
4 cups (1 L/34 fl oz) of vegetable oil

Black Vinegar Caramel
1 cup (250g/8 oz) white sugar
3 tablespoons water
½ cup (125ml/4 fl oz) black vinegar
½ tablespoon light soy sauce

Five-Spice Salt
1 tablespoon white pepper
1 tablespoon five-spice powder
3 tablespoons sea salt

Trim wing tips from chicken and discard or use to make chicken stock. Bring master stock to boil in a large saucepan or pot and add the chicken wings. Reduce to a low simmer and poach gently for 15 minutes, then let cool in stock. Remove, drain well on paper towel and refrigerate uncovered overnight.

Heat the oil in a wok and cook the wings in batches for about 5 minutes or until the skin crisps. Drain well on paper towel, keeping warm between batches in a low oven. Transfer to a serving platter and sprinkle with Five-Spice Salt. Serve with Black Vinegar Caramel as a dipping sauce.

To make five-spice salt: Grind white pepper and mix with five-spice powder and sea salt. Store in airtight container.

To make black vinegar caramel: Place sugar and water in a saucepan and bring to the boil, stirring once or twice to stop sugar sticking to the base of pan. Once the mixture starts to boil, don't stir or the sugar can re-crystallise. Keep boiling until the sugar has reached a rich golden brown colour. Very carefully, as it can splatter, add the vinegar and soy sauce. Bring back to the boil and simmer until slightly thickened. Cool and store in a clean container until needed.

If refrigerated, bring back to room temperature before using. This dipping sauce will keep for months in the fridge.

Chicken Breast with Lime, Black Beans and Ginger

Serves 4

An easy and family-friendly chicken dish using a classic combination of salted black beans and ginger.

2 tablespoons vegetable oil
4 skinless chicken breasts
2 cloves garlic, peeled and minced (ground)
2 golden shallots, peeled and thinly sliced
2 tablespoons ginger, peeled and grated
2 tablespoons salted black beans, rinsed of excess salt
4 tablespoons lime juice
2 tablespoons soy sauce
1–2 teaspoons light palm sugar
½ cup (125ml/4 fl oz) chicken stock (see page 124)
pinch of chilli powder (optional)
½ lime cut into thin slices

Heat the oil in a frypan. Gently fry the chicken breasts until almost cooked. Remove and set aside. Add the garlic, shallots and ginger to the pan, frying gently until fragrant. Add the black beans, lime juice, soy sauce, palm sugar, stock, chilli powder and lime slices. Bring to the boil and simmer for about 5 minutes. Add the chicken breasts and simmer in the sauce a few more minutes. Divide the chicken breasts between the serving plates and pour the sauce over.

Clay Pot Chicken with Exotic Mushrooms and Pak Choy

Serves 4 or 8 as part of a selection of dishes

Almost no-one in Asia has an oven, so this technique is perfect for slow cooking meat, poultry or seafood. The clay pot is not a good heat conductor, so the dish is very gently braised. Clay pots are available very cheaply in Asian supermarkets and need to be soaked well in water before using. They crack easily, but just dip the clay pot in water before putting over a flame (this recipe uses an oven). Even though the list of ingredients is extensive, most keen Asian cooks will have all of the sauces and most of the spices. Like most braised dishes, once the dish is in the pot, all the work is done.

4 chicken maryland
2 tablespoons vegetable oil
1 x 5cm (2 in) piece of cassia bark or cinnamon quill
2 pieces dried tangerine peel
1 large dried chilli
4 cardamom pods
4 star anise
2 tablespoons light palm sugar
1 tablespoon ginger, peeled and grated
4 cloves garlic, peeled and minced (ground)
4 dried shiitake mushrooms, stems removed, soaked in hot water until soft, and thinly sliced

½ cup (125ml/4 fl oz) Shaoxing wine
½ cup (125ml/4 fl oz) light soy sauce
2 tablespoons sweet soy sauce
2 tablespoons oyster sauce
2 cups (500ml/17 fl oz) water
1 bunch pak choy, washed and trimmed and sliced in half lengthways
150gm (5 oz) oyster mushrooms
150gm (5 oz) enoki mushrooms
2 green spring onions, including most of the green part, trimmed and sliced

Preheat oven to 160°C (325°F/Gas Mark 3).

Cut the chicken at the joint and remove any excess fat. Heat the oil in a frypan and cook the chicken until well browned. Place in a large clay pot or casserole dish.

In a saucepan, combine the cassia bark, tangerine peel, dried chilli, cardamom pods, star anise, palm sugar, ginger, garlic, shiitake mushrooms, Shaoxing wine, soy sauces, oyster sauce and water. Bring to the boil and simmer for 10 minutes. Pour over the chicken pieces and place in preheated oven for 1–1½ hours. Chicken should be almost falling off the bone.

Remove from the oven and add the pak choy and oyster and enoki mushrooms. Return to oven for 10 minutes or until the pak choy has wilted. Garnish with the green spring onions and serve at the table from the clay pot.

Chargrilled Duck Breast with Spicy Chiang Mai Sauce

Serves 4 or 8 as part of a selection of dishes

This is another version of a well-known Thai dish usually done with beef. Although the duck breast is covered with a rich layer of fatty skin, the meat underneath is quite lean. Careful cooking should result in crispy duck skin with moist succulent meat.

4 large duck breasts
2 tablespoons sweet soy sauce
2 tablespoons fish sauce
4 tablespoons lime juice
1–2 teaspoons white sugar
2 teaspoons galangal, peeled and grated
1 teaspoon roasted chilli powder
2 green spring onions, including some of the green part, finely sliced
2 golden shallots, peeled and sliced
1 tablespoon roasted rice powder
½ cup coriander (cilantro) leaves

Score the duck skin in a crosshatched pattern and season with the sweet soy sauce. Cook on a preheated moderate barbecue (grill), turning frequently, for about 12–15 minutes. When cooked, set aside, lightly covered with aluminum foil, and rest the meat while making the sauce.

To make sauce: Combine the fish sauce, lime juice, sugar, galangal, chilli powder, green spring onions, golden shallots and roasted rice powder in a bowl. Slice the duck breasts thinly and transfer to a serving plate, garnishing with the coriander leaves. Serve with the sauce on the side.

Barbecued Chicken with Sweet Chilli Dipping Sauce

Serves 4 or 8 as part of a selection of dishes

Barbecued (grilled) chicken is one of my favourite street food treats—slowly cooked over charcoal with crispy, smoky skin and moist, flavoursome flesh and often served with sweet chilli sauce. Coming back from north-east Thailand with Acland, our fearless and fluent tour leader, we stopped at a large produce market and a motorcycle vendor appeared. Set up on the back of his bike was a charcoal brazier for cooking chicken and all the ingredients and utensils for producing green papaya salad. Within 10 minutes we were sitting by the side of a 6-lane freeway enjoying a classic Issan dish of barbecued (grilled) chicken, green papaya salad and sticky rice. You don't get that by the side of the motorway in Australia!

1 size 16 chicken—1.6kg (2½ lb) or 4 chicken maryland
½ teaspoon white peppercorns
6 cloves garlic, peeled
4 coriander (cilantro) roots, washed and scraped
2 stalks lemongrass, bottom half only, trimmed and finely chopped
1–2 small chillies, chopped
2 teaspoons peeled fresh turmeric or pinch of powdered turmeric
4 tablespoons fish sauce
2 tablespoons soy sauce
1 tablespoon palm sugar

Sweet Chilli Dipping Sauce
½ cup (125g/4 oz) white sugar
¼ cup (60ml/2 fl oz) rice or coconut vinegar
¼ cup (60ml/2 fl oz) water
1 teaspoon salt
2 cloves garlic, peeled and crushed
¼ cup chopped coriander (cilantro) leaf and stem
2–6 small red chillies, finely chopped

Cut the chicken into pieces or, if using maryland, cut at the joint and place in a large bowl.

Grind the peppercorns in a mortar and pestle, then add the garlic, coriander root, lemongrass, chillies and turmeric and pound to a paste. Mix with the fish sauce, soy sauce and palm sugar and add marinade to chicken pieces, rubbing to coat well. Marinate overnight or for a minimum of 2 hours. Cook slowly on a preheated moderate barbecue (grill), turning often. The chicken can also be roasted in a moderate (180°C/350°F/Gas Mark 4) oven. Transfer to a plate and serve with Sweet Chilli Dipping Sauce.

To make dipping sauce: Combine sugar, vinegar, water and salt in a saucepan and bring to the boil, cooking over a high heat until the sauce has reduced by half. Stir in the garlic, coriander and chillies and remove from heat.

Meat

Apart from poultry, the most commonly cooked meat in Thailand is pork—because like poultry, pigs are easy to rear in the villages and house compounds. Beef is very expensive though popular, but it is often tough by Western standards. Recipes generally allow about 150g (5 oz/¾ cup) of meat or seafood per person, though some common sense is needed, as it depends on who's coming to dinner. Keep in mind that 150g (5 oz) of meat in Asia might feed eight people, served with lots of rice and simple vegetable dishes. If you are feeding a group of local footballers, you might need 500g (1 lb), whereas if the girls from your yoga class are coming for lunch, 100g (3½ oz) of protein each would be enough.

A good rule of thumb if you are having a dinner party is that the quantity of different meats or seafood should add up to 150–200g (5–7 oz) per person.

Beef Shin Braised with Red Dates and Shiitake Mushrooms

Serves 4–6, or 8–10 as part of a selection of dishes

This beef stew has the intense flavour of dried shiitake mushrooms plus the richness of red dates—an ideal dish for a cold winter's night. Red dates are also known as jujubes and have been cultivated in China for thousands of years. They can be dried, candied or eaten fresh and are also important in Chinese medicine where they are considered to be calming and good for circulation. Red dates can be found in Asian supermarkets. If unavailable, omit rather than substituting with the common date.

2 tablespoons vegetable oil
600g (21 oz) diced beef shin or other stewing beef
3 cloves garlic, peeled and minced (ground)
3 tablespoons ginger, peeled and minced (ground)
1 tablespoon chilli bean sauce
1 medium tomato, diced
2 tablespoons Shaoxing wine
2 tablespoons yellow rock sugar
2 tablespoons soy sauce
1 tablespoon oyster sauce
500ml (16 fl oz/2 cups) water
8 Chinese red dates
4 dried shiitake mushrooms, stems removed and soaked in boiling water until soft, then thinly sliced

In a heavy-based pot, heat the oil and brown the meat. Add the remaining ingredients and bring to the boil. Reduce to a low simmer and cook, uncovered, until the meat is tender. This will take about 2 hours if using beef shin. The sauce should be reduced and thick when finished.

Barbecued Lemongrass Pork with Sweet Chilli Dipping Sauce

Serves 4 or 8 as part of a selection of dishes

Chargrilling over charcoal is one of the most popular cooking techniques in Thailand, giving meat a distinctive smoky flavour. This marinade uses rice whisky, but don't be too fussy, any whisky or even wine will do. You don't have to make a trip to Thailand to buy the Mekong Whiskey, but it's not a bad idea. A few years ago I was sitting on the beach in southern Thailand watching the sun set and drinking Mekong Whiskey over ice with a splash of lime—and thinking that it tasted very nice. We brought a bottle home but after drinking it on the back verandah, decided it actually tastes quite foul and came to the conclusion that ambience is everything! (Thai beer still tastes good in Australia though!)

500g (1 lb) pork fillet, pork loin or leg chops
½ teaspoon white pepper
2 cloves garlic, peeled
2 coriander (cilantro) roots, washed and scraped
2 stalks lemongrass, bottom half only, outer leaves removed and finely chopped
2 green spring onions, including some of the green part, finely sliced
2 tablespoons light palm sugar
2 tablespoons fish sauce
2 tablespoons soy sauce
2 teaspoons sesame oil
1 tablespoon rice whisky, whisky or wine
2 tablespoons coconut cream

Trim sinew from the pork.

Grind the white pepper in a mortar, and then add the garlic, coriander roots and lemongrass, pounding to a paste. Transfer to a bowl and add the remaining ingredients. Pour marinade over the pork and coat well. Refrigerate for 2 hours.

Barbecue (grill) over medium heat, turning often until cooked, about 10–15 minutes depending on the cut of pork used. If using pork fillet, cut into slices, transfer to a serving plate and serve with Sweet Chilli Dipping Sauce (see page 185).

Beef Braised with Cassia and Star Anise

Serves 4 or 8 as part of a selection of dishes

This is an everyday dish that is always served with a herb salad and hot-and-sour sauce.

Cassia is related to cinnamon and is sometimes called poor man's cinnamon, as most of the ground cinnamon used throughout the world is in fact cassia. It's one of the ingredients in five-spice and, being native to China, is more authentic to use in dishes from South-East Asia than cinnamon. Cinnamon is originally from Sri Lanka, has a more delicate aroma and is a fine papery quill, whereas cassia is very hard and woody. Though cassia is preferable, there's no need to be too pedantic about it.

1 L (34 fl oz/4 cups) water
500g (1 lb) diced beef shin or other stewing cut of beef
4 cloves unpeeled garlic
1 small knob ginger, peeled and sliced
3 coriander (cilantro) roots, washed and scraped
4 star anise
1 piece of cassia bark, about 10cm (4 in)
2 tablespoons sweet soy sauce
1 tablespoon soy sauce
2 tablespoons fish sauce
1–2 teaspoons light palm sugar
2 spring onions (scallions), including some of the green part, thinly sliced

Herb Salad

generous quantity of herbs, such as mint, coriander (cilantro) and basil
a big handful of bean sprouts, raw, chopped snake beans, cucumber and wedges of Chinese cabbage

Hot and Sour Sauce

2–8 red and green small chillies, any variety
4 tablespoons lime juice
1–2 tablespoons fish sauce

Combine everything except the spring onions in a pot, bring to the boil, skimming well. Simmer, uncovered, until the beef is tender, about 1½–2 hours if using beef shin.

Transfer to a serving bowl, garnish with the spring onions and serve with the Herb Salad and Hot and Sour Sauce.

To make salad: Arrange salad ingredients on a plate.

To make sauce: Combine ingredients in a bowl and serve as dipping sauce on the side.

Sticky Pork Ribs with Honeyed Plum Sauce

Serves 4–8 as part of a selection of dishes

On my first trip to Laos, we came across a group of women selling honey. They had come into the market from small villages and the honey was still in the comb and was being strained through cloth into old bottles. It was most likely one of their few sources of income and would have been collected from wild hives—a dangerous way to make a very small amount of money.

The ribs for this dish are American-style baby back ribs. Steaming them before the final baking makes them meltingly tender. Finger bowls will be needed as this is not an elegant dish for fussy eaters!

1½ kg (3 lb) American-style baby back pork spare ribs
4 cloves garlic, peeled
1 small knob ginger, peeled and chopped
1 teaspoon five-spice powder
2 tablespoons honey
2 tablespoons soy sauce
1 tablespoon dark soy sauce
2 tablespoons Shaoxing wine
½ cup (125ml/4 fl oz) Chinese-style plum sauce
2 teaspoons sesame oil
2 tablespoons toasted sesame seeds
2 green spring onions, including some of the green part, thinly sliced

Preheat oven to 200°C (400°F/Gas Mark 6).

Cut ribs into individual pieces and steam in a bamboo steamer over a wok full of boiling water or in a Chinese tiered aluminium steamer for 30 minutes. Transfer the ribs to a shallow baking tray.

In a saucepan, combine the garlic, ginger, five-spice powder, honey, soy sauces, Shaoxing wine, plum sauce and sesame oil. Bring to the boil and simmer for 10 minutes. Pour over the ribs and toss well to coat.

Place ribs in a preheated oven and bake, turning every 10 minutes until the ribs are golden brown and just starting to char on the edges. This will take about 30–45 minutes. If the sauce starts to stick and burn during the cooking, just add a little water to the pan.

Transfer to a serving platter and sprinkle with the sesame seeds and green spring onions.

Spicy Minced Pork with Crispy Tofu

Serves 4 or 8 as part of a selection of dishes

The mention of tofu often brings to mind something bland, rubbery and tasteless. In Asia, a tofu dish can often include meat or seafood without it being listed on the menu. If you are a vegetarian it is thought you would only go to a restaurant that caters to your dietary requirements. So it can be a very confusing issue for Western vegetarians when travelling in Asia, as the restaurant owner wouldn't understand why you are in his restaurant.

I've had many dishes in Thailand listed on the menu as sizzling tofu, deep-fried tofu, silken tofu soup, just to name a few, and all included some sort of meat or seafood. This dish is usually translated as Spicy Crispy Tofu as the tofu is the primary ingredient and the meat is the seasoning. But in the West the dish sells better if the meat is the main ingredient.

2 cups (500ml/17 fl oz) vegetable oil for deep-frying
250g (8 oz) medium firm tofu cut into 2½ cm (1 in) dice
2 tablespoons extra vegetable oil
1–2 tablespoons red curry paste (see page 13)
250g (8 oz/1 cup) pork mince (ground)
2–3 tablespoons fish sauce
1 tablespoon light palm sugar
¼ cup (60ml/2 fl oz) water
4 tablespoons unsalted roasted peanuts, coarsely crushed
6 kaffir lime leaves, finely shredded
handful of coriander (cilantro) sprigs
½ red chilli, de-seeded (pitted) and shredded

Heat vegetable oil in a wok to medium and deep-fry the tofu until golden and crispy. Drain on paper towel and keep warm.

Heat extra oil in a wok or frypan and cook the red curry paste on a moderate heat for a few minutes. Add the pork mince and stir-fry until the pork is cooked. Add the fish sauce, palm sugar and water and stir-fry another minute. Add the peanuts and kaffir lime leaves and simmer until the sauce has thickened.

Transfer the tofu to a serving plate and spoon the pork and peanut sauce over it. Garnish with coriander leaves and chilli strips.

Barbecued Beef with Crispy Garlic and Green Peppercorns

Serves 4 or 8 as part of a selection of dishes

Green peppercorns are available in tins at your local supermarket or, if possible, buy imported peppercorns pickled in a light brine solution from Thailand. Fresh green peppercorns, though readily available throughout Thailand, are difficult to come by in Australia.

½ cup (125ml/4 fl oz) vegetable oil
6 cloves garlic, peeled and thinly sliced
500g (1 lb) rump steak or other good quality beef
½ teaspoon ground white pepper
2 tablespoons fish sauce
1 tablespoon soy sauce
1 tablespoon sweet soy sauce
2–3 tablespoons fresh green peppercorns, or tinned peppercorns rinsed of brine

Heat oil in a wok to moderate and fry the garlic until it turns a pale golden colour. Remove garlic with a slotted spoon and strain on paper towel.

Heat the barbecue (grill) to high and chargrill the steak until cooked to your liking. Remove and rest in a warm place for about 10 minutes.

Slice the steak thinly and place in a bowl with the pepper, fish sauce, soy sauces and green peppercorns. Toss well and transfer to a serving plate. Garnish with the fried garlic.

Pork Belly with Five-Spice Powder

Serves 4 or 8 as part of a selection of dishes

This is another everyday Chinese-influenced stew using sweet spices. The rich, fatty pork belly has always been considered a choice cut in Asia and is enjoying popularity today in modern Asian dishes. It is best eaten in small quantities due to its high fat content, but pork neck would make an excellent substitute for the belly meat. Lean pork fillet or loin is not suitable for this recipe.

3 cloves garlic, peeled
2 coriander (cilantro) roots, washed and scraped
2 tablespoons vegetable oil
1 tablespoon five-spice powder
500g (1 lb) pork belly or neck, cut into 2½ cm (1 in) dice
1 L (34 fl oz/4 cups) chicken stock (see page 124)
2 tablespoons dark soy sauce
1 tablespoon light soy sauce
2 tablespoons fish sauce
1–2 tablespoons palm sugar
coriander (cilantro) leaves to garnish

In a mortar make a paste with the garlic and coriander roots using a pestle. Heat the oil in a wok or pot and gently fry the garlic and coriander paste until just starting to colour. Add the five-spice powder and pork, stir-frying until the meat is coated with the spices. Add the stock, soy sauces, fish sauce and sugar. Bring to the boil then reduce to a simmer. Skim often and cook for about 1 hour on a low heat. Transfer to a bowl and garnish with the coriander leaves.

Spiced Lamb Cutlets with Lemongrass and Tomato Sambal

Serves 4 or 8 as part of a selection of dishes

The good quality lamb we have available here is certainly not something seen in Asia. If lamb is eaten, it's usually the stronger-tasting mutton. But for most of us in the West who have been brought up eating lamb chops or roast lamb, this dish of lightly spiced cutlets chargrilled and served with an Indonesian-style relish will be a popular addition to your barbecue (grill) repertoire.

8 lamb cutlets
1 teaspoon ground cumin
1 teaspoon ground coriander (cilantro)
black pepper to taste

Lemongrass and Tomato Sambal
2 large red chillies, de-seeded (pitted) and chopped
2–4 small red chillies, chopped (optional)
2 cloves garlic

2 stalks of lemongrass, bottom half only and outer leaves removed, then finely chopped
1 teaspoon shrimp paste, lightly roasted (see page 24)
2 tablespoons vegetable oil
2 tablespoons sweet soy sauce
2 tablespoons lime juice
1 tablespoon dark palm sugar
4 ripe tomatoes, peeled, de-seeded (pitted) and chopped
¼ cup (60ml/2 fl oz) water

To prepare lamb: Toss cutlets with the ground spices and grill (broil) on preheated oiled barbecue (grill) until cooked to your liking. Transfer to a serving plate with a bowl of Lemongrass and Tomato Sambal for dipping.

To make sambal: In a mortar, combine the chillies, garlic, lemongrass and shrimp paste. Pound to a paste.

Heat the oil to medium in a saucepan and add the paste, frying gently for a few minutes.

Add the remaining ingredients and cook, stirring well for about 5 minutes. Transfer to a bowl. Makes about 1½ cups. Keeps in the fridge for several weeks.

Desserts

When most of us go to a Thai restaurant, our expectations aren't usually too high when it comes to the dessert menu. We can usually expect sticky rice with mango, a coconut custard or sometimes deep-fried banana fritters.

In Asia, sweets play a different role—they are not served at the end of a meal but as a snack to be enjoyed between meals. The variety is quite astounding. Desserts are rarely prepared at home or in restaurants but are found at markets and are usually a speciality prepared by women trained in the art.

Common ingredients for many sweets include grated coconut, coconut milk, rice flour, cooked sticky rice, tapioca and tapioca flour, mung beans and mung bean starch, eggs and different varieties of palm sugar. Bananas are often used, along with other strongly flavoured fruits such as mango, jackfruit and durian.

The textural component of Thai sweets can sometimes be challenging to a Western palate; textures are often gluey and sticky from the starches used, while the addition of ingredients like sweet corn, black beans or fried shallots may seem at odds with the concept of sweets.

Over 15 years at the Spirit House restaurant, the most popular desserts have always been the more familiar European styles executed with an Asian sensibility, rather than the more traditional Thai sweet snacks. The following recipes are a mixture of traditional and modern Asian.

Ginger Coconut Caramel Custards

Serves 8

This is an Asian take on a classic crème caramel, so rather than the dense traditional custard made with coconut milk, this recipe uses milk and cream infused with toasted coconut for a more delicate silken texture. The custards are best made the day before.

Caramel
2 cups (500g/1 lb) sugar
½ cup (125ml/4 fl oz) water

Custard
1 cup coconut, shredded and toasted
1 cup ginger, peeled and roughly chopped
500ml (17 fl oz/2 cups) cream
500ml (17 fl oz/2 cups) milk
6 whole eggs
200g (7 oz/1 cup) sugar

8 x 175ml (5½ fl oz) dariole moulds (available in any kitchenware shop)

To make caramel: Place sugar and ¼ cup (60ml/2 fl oz) water in a saucepan and gently dissolve the sugar, stirring only once or twice. Increase to a high heat and cook without stirring until the sugar has turned a rich golden caramel. Add remaining ¼ cup (60ml/2 fl oz) water and return to heat to dissolve. Pour into the base of the dariole moulds to a depth of 1cm (½ in). Allow to set.

To make custard: In a saucepan, combine the coconut, ginger, cream and milk. Bring to just below boiling point, then remove from heat. Cover and allow to infuse for 30 minutes. Strain and squeeze as much liquid from the coconut mixture as possible and add extra milk to make up 1 litre (1³/4 pints) of liquid.

In a bowl, lightly whisk the eggs and sugar and add to the strained milk. Whisk to combine. Take care not to over-whisk. Strain mixture into a bowl or large jug. Strain again and then pour on top of the set caramel, dividing equally between the dariole moulds.

To bake caramel custards: Place the dariole moulds in a large baking tray half filled with hot water and bake in a preheated 170°C (325°F/Gas Mark 3) oven for 30 minutes, or until just set. Remove from oven and leave in the water bath to cool down. Refrigerate overnight before unmoulding. Serve with a dollop of cream and seasonal fruit.

Coconut Rice Pudding with Toffee Crust and Mango Sauce

Serves 6

During a winter baking frenzy, I decided to make my son a treat of old-fashioned rice pudding like my Nanna made. Having travelled and eaten extensively throughout South-East Asia while growing up, Liam enjoyed a multitude of Asian sweets, but especially loved sticky rice with coconut cream. I had to laugh at his surprise on tasting my Nanna's version. He thought the texture was weird and the flavour insipid—can't win all the time.

The following recipe is a bit of a fusion between the two. The typical Thai sweet, salty and creamy notes are present, but the use of jasmine instead of sticky rice lightens the texture somewhat. A dollop of vibrant tangy mango sauce offsets the richness.

2 cups (500ml/17 fl oz) milk
1 cup (250ml/8 fl oz) coconut milk
1 cinnamon stick
1 vanilla bean, split and seeds scraped
1 teaspoon salt
1¼ cups jasmine rice, washed and drained well
1 cup (250g/8 oz) white sugar
1¼ cups (300ml/10 fl oz) cream
1 teaspoon lime zest

Mango Sauce
2 mangoes
2–3 tablespoons white sugar
1 tablespoon lime juice

In a saucepan, combine the milk, coconut milk, cinnamon stick, vanilla bean and salt. Bring to the boil and add the rice. Stir to prevent sticking and turn the heat down to very low. Cook, uncovered, until all the liquid has been absorbed, about 30 minutes. Remove from the heat and stir in $^2/_3$ cup of the sugar. Set aside to cool completely.

Whisk the cream to soft peaks and fold into the cooled rice mixture along with the lime zest. Remove the vanilla bean and cinnamon stick and then divide the rice between 6 serving bowls. Sprinkle the remaining sugar over the top of the rice and caramelise with a blowtorch or under a very hot griller (broiler). Serve with a dollop of mango sauce on top.

To make sauce: Remove cheeks from 1 mango and dice very finely. Remove remaining mango flesh from both mangoes and chop roughly, then puree in a blender with the white sugar and lime juice. Mix the diced and pureed mango together.

Tapioca Pudding with Palm Sugar Sauce

Serves 6–8

Let's start with one ingredient that always polarises palates— tapioca. I love it! This is the perfect example of an ingredient with texture but no flavour. Fruits like banana or mango can be served with this pudding and the tapioca takes on the rich caramel flavour from the palm sugar syrup together with the richness of coconut cream.

8 cups (2 L/67 fl oz) water
1 cup tapioca or sago
200g (7 oz/1 cup) dark palm sugar (Pontiac brand from Indonesia if available), chopped
150ml (5 fl oz/²/3 cup) water
200ml (7 fl oz/³/4 cup) thick coconut milk or cream
½ teaspoon salt
2 tablespoons fresh coconut, shredded (optional)

Bring water to the boil and add the tapioca, stirring well to stop the grains clumping together. Simmer until just translucent, about 5 to 10 minutes, then strain, rinsing well under cold water. Divide between serving bowls, then pour over the palm sugar sauce, followed by the coconut sauce. Garnish with shredded coconut.

To make palm sugar sauce: Combine the chopped palm sugar and water in a saucepan and bring to the boil. Simmer until the sugar has dissolved. Cool before using.

To make coconut sauce: Gently warm the coconut milk with the salt until dissolved. Cool before using.

Five-Spice Honey Panna Cotta with Poached Peaches and Fresh Berries

Serves 8

Panna cotta is a versatile dessert and once the technique is understood it can be adapted to many flavours. This recipe is ideal to showcase fabulous summer peaches. The warm spices in the panna cotta would work with a wide variety of fruits.

2 cinnamon sticks
4 star anise
6 cardamom pods
4 cloves
½ teaspoon Szechuan pepper
400ml (14 fl oz/1¾ cups) milk
400ml (14 fl oz/1¾ cups) cream
4 leaves gelatine
100g (3½ oz/½ cup) caster sugar
1½ tablespoons honey
mixed berries, such as strawberries, raspberries washed

Poached Peaches
8 ripe peaches
500g (1 lb/2 cups) white sugar
500ml (17 fl oz/2 cups) water
1 cup (250ml/8 fl oz) white wine
1 strip lemon zest
1 cinnamon stick
1 vanilla bean

Dry-roast the spices over a low heat until fragrant. Place in a clean tea towel and then crush coarsely with a rolling pin. Put the bruised spices in a saucepan with the milk and heat gently for 10 minutes without letting it come to the boil. Remove from heat, cover and allow to infuse for at least 2 hours in the refrigerator, or preferably overnight.
Whip the cream until soft peaks form. Soak the gelatine in cold water for about a minute until it softens, then squeeze out excess water. Strain the infused milk into a saucepan along with the sugar and honey. Heat gently until the sugar has dissolved. Stir in the softened gelatine. Transfer to a bowl and place the bowl in a larger bowl that has been filled with ice and water. Stir until the mixture is on the verge of setting. Fold in the whipped cream and then transfer to 8 dariole moulds or ramekin dishes. Refrigerate until set.

To make poached peaches: Place sugar and water in a saucepan and stir until the sugar is dissolved. Add the wine, lemon zest, cinnamon and vanilla bean. Simmer a few minutes, then add the peaches. Press a piece of baking paper onto the surface of the syrup and poach fruit gently for about 5 minutes. Remove from syrup with a slotted spoon. Skin fruit and transfer to a bowl. Reduce syrup by half and, when cool, pour over peaches.

To serve, remove panna cotta gently from moulds onto each serving plate, place a poached peach on the plate with a drizzle of the poaching liquid then garnish with a scattering of mixed berries.

Pineapple and Lemongrass Granita

Serves 6–8

Granitas are an easy alternative to sorbets as they don't need an ice-cream maker. Just about any fruit can be used. Serve with fresh fruit for a refreshing summer dessert.

½ cup (125g/4 oz) sugar
½ cup (125ml/4 fl oz) water
3 stalks lemongrass, one or two layers removed, crushed and roughly chopped
1 large sweet pineapple, juiced to extract about 400ml (14 fl oz/1¾ cups)
2 tablespoons lime juice
pineapple, thinly sliced, for garnish

Combine the sugar and water in a small saucepan and bring to the boil. Add the lemongrass and simmer for about 5 minutes. Remove from heat and let sit for half an hour. Strain sugar syrup, pressing down well on the lemongrass to extract as much flavour as possible, and then discard the lemongrass. Mix together the sugar syrup, pineapple juice and lime juice. Pour into a shallow metal tray and place in the freezer. As the mixture starts to set, flake with a fork, repeating every 45 minutes until frozen. Best served on the day it's made.

Young Coconut and Lime Sorbet

Serves 6

A generous scoop of this refreshing and tangy sorbet with seasonal fruit such as mango or sweet red papaya would be the perfect finish for a rich, spicy meal. Young coconut water can be bought in cans from good supermarkets or you may even find young drinking coconuts in your local fruit and vegetable shop. Just cut the top off and use the juice inside.

zest of 2 limes
175g (5¾ oz/¾ cup) white sugar
100ml (3 fl oz/½ cup) water
500ml (17 fl oz/2 cups) young coconut juice
125ml (4 fl oz/½ cup) fresh lime juice
2 tablespoons Malibu liquor

Combine the lime zest, sugar and water in a saucepan and bring to the boil, simmer for 5 minutes on a low heat and strain. Discard the lime zest and cool. Stir in the coconut water and lime juice. Transfer to ice-cream machine and churn until frozen, adding the Malibu during the last 10 minutes of churning.

Alternatively, this can be made into a granita by pouring into a shallow dish and freezing. Every 45 minutes use a fork to scrape the mixture until it's a frozen slush. This will need to be done about 5–6 times. Best used within 24 hours.

Steamed Ginger Pudding with Star Anise Anglaise

Serves 6

This is a traditional old-fashioned steamed pudding, but Spirit House chef Kelly Lord has given it a more vibrant spicing with the addition of star anise. It has always been a winter favourite on the restaurant menu.

Ginger Pudding
300g (10 oz) candied ginger
80g (2½ oz) golden syrup
40ml (1½ fl oz/2 tablespoons) ginger wine
40g (1½ oz) glucose syrup
4 eggs, separated
80g (2½ oz/¼ cup) sugar
20g (1 oz) butter
200ml (7 fl oz/1 cup) milk
300g (10 oz) self-raising flour

Star Anise Anglaise
200ml (7 fl oz/1 cup) milk
4 star anise
100ml (3½ fl oz/½ cup) pouring cream
4 egg yolks
90g (3 oz/½ cup) sugar

To make ginger pudding: Blend candied ginger, golden syrup, ginger wine and glucose syrup together and set aside.

Whisk egg yolks and sugar until pale, add butter to egg mix, then add ginger mix.

Fold milk and flour into the mix. Whisk egg whites to a stiff peak and fold through mixture.

Spoon into buttered dariole moulds three-quarters deep, and bake in a water bath in a preheated moderate oven (180°C/350°F/Gas Mark 4) for 30 minutes. Remove from oven and stand in moulds for 10–15 minutes before turning out.

To make anglaise: Place milk, star anise and cream in a pot and bring to a simmer.

Whisk egg yolks and sugar together and add warm milk.

Place into a clean pot and cook on a low heat, stirring constantly until mixture thickens and coats the back of a wooden spoon. Remove from heat and strain into a clean bowl to cool.

To serve, divide the Star Anise Anglaise between 6 serving bowls and then place the puddings in the centre of the anglaise on each plate.

Coconut Pancakes with Pandanus Ice-cream

Serves 8

Pancakes are a backpacker favourite throughout Asia, served with a huge selection of toppings and fillings. I like to stick to the more traditional flavours such as coconut, banana or lime juice with sugar, and leave the Nutella and chocolate syrup to the more adventurous young travellers.

Pandanus leaf is used to flavour both sweet and savoury dishes in Asia. Usually any sweet that's coloured green is pandanus flavoured. The essence can be bought in good Asian supermarkets without the green food colouring if preferred, along with the frozen leaves.

Coconut Pancakes
250g (8 oz) plain flour
½ teaspoon salt
2 eggs
1 cup (250ml/8 fl oz) coconut milk
2 cups (500ml/17 fl oz) milk
butter for frying

Pancake Filling
100g (3½ oz/½ cup) dark palm sugar, chopped
½ cup (125ml/4 fl oz) water
1 cup fresh coconut, shredded

To make pancakes: Sift the flour and salt into a bowl. In a separate bowl whisk together the eggs, coconut milk and milk. Pour the egg mixture into the flour, stirring to make a thin batter. Strain through a sieve and set aside, covered, for 2 hours.

Heat a crepe pan or small frypan to medium and add a little butter. Pour in a thin stream of batter and swirl to coat the pan. Cook for a few minutes until set. Turn out onto a plate and repeat with remaining batter. This quantity should make 16 pancakes.

To make filling: Combine the palm sugar and water in a small saucepan and simmer until the sugar has dissolved. Stir in the shredded coconut.

To serve, allow 2 pancakes per person and divide the coconut filling between the pancakes. Place on a serving plate with a scoop of Pandanus Ice-cream (see page 219).

Pandanus Ice-cream

Serves 8

1 cup (250ml/8 fl oz) cream
1 cup (250ml/8 fl oz) milk
3 whole pandanus leaves tied in a knot
5 egg yolks
100g (3½ oz/½ cup) sugar
pandanus essence to taste

Bring the cream, milk and pandanus leaves to just below the boil. Remove from heat and allow to infuse, covered, for half an hour.

Whisk together the egg yolks and sugar, then add the pandanus essence. Add to the cream and milk mixture, stirring to combine.

Place the bowl over a saucepan of simmering water and cook, stirring constantly until the mixture coats the back of a spoon. Strain and chill completely in the fridge before churning in an ice-cream machine according to the manufacturer's instructions.

Index

First published in Australia in 2010 by
New Holland Publishers (Australia) Pty Ltd
Sydney • Auckland • London • Cape Town

www.newholland.com.au

1/66 Gibbes Street Chatswood NSW 2067 Australia
218 Lake Road Northcote Auckland New Zealand
86 Edgware Road London W2 2EA United Kingdom
80 McKenzie Street Cape Town 8001 South Africa

National Library of Australia Cataloguing-in-Publication entry

Fear, Annette,
Essentially Thai/Spirit House/Annette Fear, Helen Brierty.

ISBN: 9781741108583(hbk)
Cookery, Thai.
Other Authors/Contributors: Brierty, Helen.

641.59593

Publisher: Fiona Schultz
Publishing manager: Lliane Clarke
Project editor: Helen McGarry
Editor: Geraldine Coren
Photography: Graeme Gillies/NHIL
Cover photograph: Graeme Gillies/NHIL
Proofreader: Nina Paine
Designer: Tania Gomes
Production manager: Olga Dementiev
Printer: Toppan Leefung Printing Ltd (China)